The
Wealth of Information

By the same author:

NUCLEAR DISASTER

The
Wealth of
Information

**A PROFILE OF
THE POST-INDUSTRIAL ECONOMY**

TOM STONIER

Thames Methuen

First published in Great Britain 1983 by
Methuen London Ltd
11 New Fetter Lane, London EC4P 4EE
in association with
Thames Television International
149 Tottenham Court Road, London W1P 9LL
Reprinted 1983, 1985
Copyright © 1983 Tom Stonier

British Library Cataloguing in Publication data:

Stonier, Tom
    The wealth of information.
    1. Great Britain – Economic conditions – 18th century
    2. Great Britain – Economic conditions – 19th century
    3. Great Britain – Economic conditions – 20th century
    4. Great Britain – Economic policy
    I. Title
    330.941   HC255

    ISBN 0-423-00620-7
    ISBN 0-423-00800-5 Pbk

Printed in Great Britain by Butler & Tanner Ltd
Frome and London

Contents

This book is dedicated to my father, John Stonier, who taught me to care for the world.

Prologue: Adam Smith

'The annual labour of every nation is the fund which originally supplies it with all the necessaries and conveniences of
life which it annually consumes, and which consists always
either in the immediate produce of that labour, or in what is
purchased with that produce from other nations.'

Adam Smith, Introduction.

With these words Adam Smith introduced the reader to his
monumental work *The Wealth of Nations*. It was at a time, a little
over two centuries ago, when society was changing rapidly,
socially and economically. Towards the end of the eighteenth
century, agriculture was still dominant – the ownership of land
was of prime importance, the vast bulk of the labour force was
still working on farms – it is no wonder that many were dazzled
by the pre-eminence of the agricultural sector of the economy.
Yet, in retrospect, we can see that the economy in Smith's day
was beginning to slip into a 'post-agricultural' economy. In
Queen Victoria's heyday, under the pressure of advancing technology, Great Britain had shifted to an industrial economy.
From an exporter of food, she had become a net importer.
Political power had shifted from the landed aristocrat to the
capitalist. The bulk of the labour force was no longer employed
on the land. Manufacture and trade, not agriculture, accounted
for the biggest share of the country's productive potential.

Today we have witnessed a similar shift. From a major exporter of manufactured goods, the United Kingdom has become
an importer. Political power is shifting from the owners of
capital to the professional bureaucrats and technocrats – the
purveyors of information. Only a shrinking minority of the
labour force toils in factories; and the service sector has overtaken manufacture in terms of the country's gross national
product. We now live in a post-industrial economy.

This book explores two major concepts. The first is the economic importance of information. Information has upstaged land, labour and capital as the most important input into modern productive systems. Information reduces the requirement for land, labour and capital. It reduces the requirements for raw materials and energy. It spawns entire new industries. It is sold in its own right, and it is the raw material for the fastest growing sector of the economy – the knowledge industry. The labour market is now dominated by information operatives who make their living by virtue of the fact that they possess the information needed to get things done.

The second major point is that government spending, by and large, is not consumption, but either involves the purchase of services vital to the economy or represents investment. The business and industrial community, as well as the public at large, needs to understand that the government is the biggest creator, co-ordinator and provider of information. It is also the most important investor in the future of the economy. The increasing percentage of the gross domestic product spent by the governments of all western countries reflects not profligacy, but is a natural economic consequence of post-industrial society.

This book attempts to clarify the relationship between information and money in a qualitative way so that it becomes possible to formulate sound policies at all levels of the economy – the quantitative theory must wait.

1 On wealth, value and information

As the title implies, this book is concerned with the concept of wealth and how to create it. Three or four centuries ago, people thought of wealth primarily as gold and silver. One of the most articulate exponents of this idea was a rich English merchant, Thomas Mun. To increase the wealth of a nation, England must sell to other countries more than she bought from them. Mun had other ideas about increasing national wealth: cultivate unused lands, be frugal in the use of natural resources, develop industries at home to supply necessities, avoid frivolous changes in fashion, reduce the consumption of foreign products. When selling abroad, carry English goods in English ships, cut prices on goods with strong competition but hold dear prices on goods which you monopolise, make England a centre for exchange between the products of other nations, buy as close to the source as possible to avoid middlemen, and place no restriction on outflow of gold or money used for overseas investment, for like farmers who appear to be wasting good food when they scatter seeds on the ground, the overseas investments will reap a harvest many times over. Not bad for early seventeenth-century thinking.

That only silver and gold constituted wealth was a concept already being challenged early in the seventeenth century by Antoine de Montchetrien. To him, wealth was not only money but also commodities necessary to sustain life. Montchetrien chided his countrymen for importing goods which could be made at home and emphasised domestic trade over foreign exchange. The chief function of government, as far as he was concerned, was to assure that a sufficient quantity of the basic necessities were available for all.

By the eighteenth and nineteenth centuries the mercantilist school of thought held that wealth included all kinds of produce, agricultural and manufactured, although according to some, a nation's wealth consisted only of those products originating within the country.

The father of the eighteenth-century group of economists known as the physiocrats, François Quesnay, described a nation's wealth not in the amount of money it can hoard, but in the amount of raw material it can make available to satisfy human requirements. Wealth, according to Quesnay, is created by the surplus of agricultural and mineral products after deducting the cost of production. Manufacturing does not create wealth, it merely reworks the same materials: the increase in value of a manufactured item reflects the utilisation and consumption of other materials (iron, food for the workers, etc.) necessary for the productive process. In a similar vein, Quesnay considered that commerce does not create wealth – it merely redistributes it.

It is against this background that Adam Smith wrote, in part at least, to correct some of the physiocrats' ideas. To Smith, wealth was the sum of all exchange values which an individual or a nation possessed. This included a person's labour. Unlike the physiocrats, Smith emphasised that other forms of labour besides mining and agriculture were productive.

He then went on to formulate his labour theory of value: the value of an object is equal to the quantity of labour it can demand in exchange for itself: 'Labour alone, therefore, never varying in its own intrinsic value, is alone the ultimate and real standard by which the value of all commodities can at all times and places be estimated and compared. It is their real price; money is their nominal price only.' (Adam Smith, Book One, Chapter V.)

Smith believed that wealth was built up by industry and frugality, both at an individual and at a national level. This idea that the nation's wealth, like that of an individual, is increased by savings was criticised by some of Smith's contemporaries and by those who followed him. For example, John Rae considered that while individuals grow rich by acquiring a larger portion of wealth already in existence, nations grow wealthy by creating new wealth. Rae placed great emphasis on invention as a major mechanism of wealth creation and argued for the protection of infant industries. To some extent, the importance of technology in wealth creation was also implied in Smith's writing. For although his attention was focussed on the importance of labour in creating wealth, his emphasis on the division of labour as being of utmost importance reflected the emerging factory system of his time and the advancing technology leading to the Industrial Revolution.

Some of the continental economists of the early nineteenth century, such as the German economist, Friedrich List, asserted that the well-being of a country is based on the development of productive powers rather than by the accumulation of wealth. List considered these productive powers to include science, law, government, religion and art. Teachers, physicians, judges and administrators, according to List, may not produce wealth directly, but they do develop the productive powers of the state. In a similar vein, the French populariser of Adam Smith, Jean Baptiste Say, included in the wealth of a nation immaterial products such as the performance of a musician. Why should not talent be considered as wealth?

In addition to the concept of wealth, there is the closely related question of what makes an item or service valuable. This is a minefield of subjective evaluation and theories. John Locke believed that labour determined value. Locke considered land, as such, valueless – it was the application of labour which caused it to yield. Capital was labour stored up in tools and equipment. This concept was reinforced early in the nineteenth century by David Ricardo, while early socialists such as William Thompson also proclaimed that machinery was stored-up labour, as did Marx.

An idea which would have been new to all these thinkers is that tools and machinery may be stored-up labour, but they are also, and more significantly, stored-up information! This is true for capital, the productivity of land and any other aspect of economics which invokes stored labour. There exists no productive labour inputs which do not, at the same time, involve inputs of information. Furthermore, information, like capital, can be accumulated and stored for future use. In a post-industrial society, a country's store of information is its principal asset, its greatest potential source of wealth.

There are three major ways by which a society increases its wealth significantly: 1. by the slow and steady accumulation of capital; 2. through military conquest or other territorial expansion; and 3. by means of new technology which converts 'non-resources' into 'resources'. Because of the advanced state of technology in post-industrial economies, the conversion of 'non-resources' into useful products has become the basic principle of new wealth creation: oil under the North Sea and desert land reclamation are two such examples.

At the base of advanced technology is knowledge, especially advanced science. Unlike earlier times when practical experience laid the foundation for new science, the flow of information is now generally in the opposite direction. For example, in the nineteenth century, the experience with the steam engine led to the science of thermodynamics. In contrast, the development of the transistor in the middle of the twentieth century was dependent on the solid-state physics conducted decades earlier.

People create wealth. Human capital is the most important resource of post-industrial societies. It is through technological expertise and organisational competence that new, wealth-creating systems come into existence. Technological expertise and managerial competence need to be backed up by a skilled labour force to implement the development of new systems. In addition to these skills, the development of new productive systems also requires a very different kind of skill. This is a form of business acumen which understands market opportunities and how to exploit them. It is the assured sale of a product or service which motivates its development. This is true even if it is a charitable or government-run enterprise.

EDUCATION AND WEALTH CREATION

At the base of all skills, competence and expertise is education. In its broadest sense, education includes the accumulation of information by an individual, including practical experience.

The best strategy to effect a smooth transition from an industrial to an information economy is by means of a massive expansion of both education, and research and development. The latter should be aimed at creating the wealth necessary to support expansion of the public service sector (government-run) economy. The expansion of the former, education, is required to upgrade the human capital to make the workforce economically more productive, ranging from manual labour to theoretical scientist; to create an informed citizenry capable of manoeuvring effectively in an information economy; and to keep everybody from going neurotic in a rapidly changing information environment.

We will need a whole new cradle-to-grave system which includes community education for the mature. In a rapidly changing information environment, people will need to move in and out of education throughout their lives. Life-styles will change, with periods of paid employment alternating with periods of education and with leisure activities.

The question of the precise value of new knowledge and education to the economy as a whole is a most difficult and vexing question. Take, for example, the fairly traditional approach by E. F. Denison. Denison looks at all the factors he can think of which would increase the growth of an economy. He then assigns a value to them. The sum of these is not quite up to the actual growth observed. The difference, the 'residual', is attributed to growth in knowledge. According to Denison, about half of the average annual growth rate in the United States between 1929 and 1957 is directly attributable to an increase in the dissemination or creation of information.

His calculations are interesting; they represent the serious and laudable efforts of a scholar to provide quantitative values for a system poorly understood. They probably greatly underestimated the input of new information, directly or indirectly, into the system, since they include so many assumptions; and there is no reason to believe that his analysis, however numerical, is accurate.

Until there appears an Einstein of economics who can quan-

tify the relationship between information, productivity and
other economic factors, it is probably reasonable to consider
that most of the growth in national product is attributable to
advances in expertise and technology. There exists no human
activity, and certainly no economic activity, which directly or
indirectly does not have an information component.

SINGAPORE: A CASE STUDY

A classic example of the importance of applied knowledge is
provided by the remarkable economic growth of the tiny Asian
island state of Singapore. It is a country which prospers not
because it is rich, but because it is smart. Singapore has probably
the most successful 'planned' economy in the world. Between
1970 and 1979 its economy grew, on average, at an annual rate
of 7.3 per cent, so that by the end of the decade it ended up with
a *per capita* income of $US3,187 (1979). An outstanding per-
formance for any country.

In the early 1960s the emphasis in Singapore was on import
substitution. By means of high tariff protection it nurtured a
variety of industries which would reduce the dependence on
imports. The focus on import substitution became replaced, in
due course, with an emphasis on export-oriented manufacturing. This required foreign capital and technology. The Singapore Economic Development Board, already established in
1961, went after the multinational corporations as 'the best
equipped institutions to provide modern technology and quality
control'. Generous investment incentives made it profitable to
establish various export-oriented manufacturing industries, and
the same kinds of incentives were also used to induce the world's
leading banks and other institutions to revitalise and expand
the financial centres built up during Singapore's earlier entrepôt
days. In addition, in spite of anti-colonial feelings against serv-
ing foreigners, a tourist industry was established with hotels, car
rental agencies, shopping arcades, cultural events, courteous
customs inspectors and so forth.

In 1965, the year of Singapore's independence, it had about
a thousand manufacturing firms employing about 47,000

workers, producing $US360 million worth of goods. Fifteen years later there were 3,347 firms employing 287,314 workers producing $US16,400 million. With this sort of rapid economic growth, full employment was reached in the mid-1970s, and labour became in short supply. Both in response to this situation, and as part of a deliberate policy to encourage mechanisation and automation, the National Wages Council recommended substantial 'corrective' wage increases, essentially more pay for more skilled work. The increased wages policy became part of the 'Ten-Year Economic Development Plan' and is designed to break the vicious circle of low wages sustaining labour-intensive industries which, in turn, tend to favour low productivity, an over-tight labour market and economic stagnation.

'The purpose of the exercise,' stated Dr Goh Keng Swee, First Deputy Prime Minister, 'is not to give more pay for the same work, neither more pay for less work. It is more pay for better work and more skilled work.'

Mr Goh Chock Tong, Minister for Trade and Industry, recognised that the key to the long-term success of economic restructuring was workforce development. Accordingly, the National University of Singapore admitted 40 per cent more engineering students in 1980, while the two technical colleges increased their enrolment by 11 per cent. Similarly, the Joint Industrial Training Centres expanded their classes by 32 per cent, while a Skills Development Fund gave employers grants to train over 10,000 workers.

'Our aim is modest,' said Goh, the Minister for Trade and Industry, '... to step into the shoes left behind by countries like Germany and Japan as they restructure, they from skill-intensive to knowledge-intensive industries and we from labour-intensive to skill-intensive industries.'

Research and development (R & D) is expected to play a vital role in the restructuring of the economy. The government considers:

While some of the best and most profitable industrial R & D work is and should be done by the firms themselves, there are many industrial problems which are most economically done on behalf of firms at central laboratories. The providing of technical support and testing services by the Singapore Institute of Standards and Industrial Research (SISIR) assists many firms, especially the smaller ones, to adopt and modify their capital equipment, improve their productivity, develop their quality control systems, and to upgrade their products to standards acceptable by foreign markets.

Toward this end, Singapore is opening a 136-hectare Science Park to pure R & D organisations and high-technology firms which need to engage in industrial R & D (as well as manufacture). The first phase will be ready for occupancy in 1983.

Commenting on the Ten-Year Economic Development Plan, Minister Goh explained:

> If we succeed we shall be manufacturing high technology products like integrated circuits, computers, industrial electronic equipment, aircraft components, numerical-control machine tools, medical instruments like X-ray machines and blood counters, and specialty pharmaceutical products. To realise our objectives we require more engineers, accountants, lawyers, doctors, skilled workers and other managerial and professional personnel. We shall train them. We shall also induct talent from abroad.

Mr Yeo Seng Teck, director of the Economic Development Board, summed up the government's motivation: 'Our philosophy is simple. Since we have no natural resources nor a large domestic market, we have no choice but to depend on export-oriented manufacturing for our continuing growth and, indeed, for our economic survival.'

1980 was not a good year for the economy of most OECD countries. Singapore's economy, on the other hand, grew by 10.2 per cent. One gets the distinct impression that the Singapore political leaders have a much clearer view of what is going on in the world than do their European, especially their British, counterparts.

Traditional economic thinking would attribute much, if not

most, of Singapore's economic growth to a massive inflow of finance capital. No doubt this capital inflow was a necessary factor in Singapore's growth. It was not, however, a sufficient condition. It was not even the major factor. The world is not short of finance capital. What it is short of is the information needed to employ that capital to maximum advantage. It must be apparent that the state of Singapore was led by a top-notch management team which knew how to put together a unique combination of land (very little), labour (relatively unskilled) and capital, to yield highly productive industries. The economic boom which Singapore experienced in the 1970s was no accident: it was the product of imagination and expertise. To claim that most of this dramatic growth reflected inputs of capital is like saying that Einstein created the Theory of Relativity because he ate a good breakfast. The concepts people have in their heads, and the quality of the information available to them, determines the success or failure of an enterprise. Know-how is the limiting factor in wealth creation.

ON INFORMATION

'Value-added' is a term generally applied to some material or service which has been worked over in such a way that the final product is more valuable than the original. For example, wool converted into cloth is more valuable, pound for pound, than unprocessed wool. The value added is achieved by taking the original material, wool (which is itself a product) and adding further inputs of labour, capital (in the form of plant and machinery), energy and land (for factory sites). Information, however, is a major input - and one which is usually ignored!

The process of converting wool into cloth requires information at each step. The fibres in the original fleece are rearranged by combing and carding, then by spinning the wool into yarn. Second, the yarn is woven into patterns. The process of weaving involves an input of information in the form of a pattern or a design. It takes skill and know-how to spin, weave or operate power machinery and operatives need training.

Last, there is the information input into the whole process

itself. The wool industry, in order to exist, is based on the general insight that it is possible to convert the hair on a sheep into woven cloth. At each step in the process, in particular each mechanical device or piece of machinery, has as an intrinsic part of it an accumulation of information.

Every machine contains within it a history of innovation and invention. This accumulation of information is as important as the accumulation of capital.

Any object or material can be made more valuable by adding information: waste desert land plus information becomes productive crop land. Ignorant labourers plus education become skilled, highly productive operatives. Idle capital plus information becomes revenue-yielding investment. Useless energy like sunshine or ocean waves can be made to perform useful work when you know how. The reason why education, as an industry, continues to command an ever-increasing share of the nation's wealth (ignoring minor and temporary government cuts) is because education adds information to people, thereby increasing their economic value. Over the next few decades education will grow to become the largest industry in the post-industrial society and its number one employer.

We need to develop a whole new field of economics: information economics. What is the value added to an object, material, person or process upon the addition of information? Information, as an entity in its own right, has some peculiar properties. For example, if I have a thousand acres of land and I give you 500 to use for your own, then I cannot use more than 500 acres for myself. If I have two sausages and I give you one, presumably you will eat it, and I have only one sausage left. But if I have a body of information and I let you use half of it, I can still use all I've got. Whereas the use of land or material goods, energy or labour, is such that if I let you have some, I diminish my own holdings, this is not necessarily the case for information. In fact, if I let you use my information it is quite likely that you will turn up something quite useful which helps me. Whereas material transactions can lead to competition, information transactions are much more likely to lead to cooperation – information is a resource which can be truly shared.

Another strange feature relates to the consumption of information. In general, the consumption of material or energy causes an increase in the entropy of the universe. Entropy is a sort of mathematical disorganisation. Consuming information does the opposite. It adds to the store of an individual's information, increases organisation and decreases entropy. Unlike driving a car, or eating a sausage, a book is not diminished by being read. Only the mechanical act of turning the pages wears it out, not by having its contents read.

Information can add value not only to the other inputs such as land or labour; it can add value to itself. 'Data' is a series of disconnected facts and observations. These may be converted to 'information' by analysing, cross-referring, selecting, sorting, summarising or in some other way organising the data. It takes work to convert data into information. Information is more valuable than data; it is data transformed into a meaningful guide for specific purposes. Patterns of information in turn can be worked up into a coherent body of 'knowledge'. Knowledge consists of an organised body of information, such information patterns forming the basis of insights and judgements.

Consider the analogy of converting fleece into yarn, then weaving the yarn into cloth. The fleece is equivalent to data, the yarn to information and the cloth to knowledge. Just as a loom can weave strands of yarn into patterns of cloth, so can a computer weave strands of information into patterns of knowledge. The computer is, itself, an information machine and an example of information adding value to information.

The terms 'data', 'information' and 'knowledge' have been used somewhat loosely in this book. This is because what is information at one level may only be data at the next. For example, interviewing a person can yield valuable information to an interviewer. However, that same information becomes a mere datum for a census. The information provided by the census may represent mere data for a further analysis leading to a more sophisticated projection which in turn becomes mere data for making policy decisions.

There is no substitute for hard data. On the other hand, as Emanuel Kant is quoted as saying, there is nothing so practical as a good theory. A good theory is a device to help predict and organise facts. In the latter capacity it helps to add value to new information. If that new information adds a lot of value to some new material, then a good theory can be worth a lot of money. Solid-state physics theories helped organise the facts necessary for developing silicon into transistors. Transistors produced miracle chips and photovoltaic cells.

The great intellectual problem confronting economics today is to quantify the impact of information on the economy and to translate this paramount factor into monetary terms.

2 What is a post-industrial economy?

'No large country, it must be observed, ever did or could subsist without some sort of manufactures being carried on in it ...'

Adam Smith, Book Three, Chapter III.

INTRODUCTION

Smith's statement is as true two centuries later as when he wrote it. However, the emphasis has shifted. Just as in Smith's day the economy was beginning to shift from agriculture to manufacturing, so today there is a shift from manufacturing to information. Just as the late eighteenth and nineteenth centuries saw a shift to a post-agricultural economy, so has the technologically advanced sector of global society shifted to a post-industrial economy.

In the agrarian economy, the economy was concerned primarily with producing enough food and the limiting factor usually was the availability of good land. In the industrial economy, the economy was geared to the production of goods and the limiting factor tended to be capital. In an information economy, the economy is concerned with the creating and application of information to make all forms of production more efficient and to create new wealth. The limiting factor tends to be existing knowledge.

KNOWLEDGE IS A LIMITING FACTOR

The production of goods and services required to fulfil our personal or community needs is subject to different limiting factors at different times. Following the Great Plague of the fourteenth century in Europe, there was a great labour shortage. All sorts of economic and political consequences flowed from that economic fact; among these a natural rise in wages.

By the end of the fifteenth century, the population expanded rapidly – so did the prices of foodstuffs. Wages failed to keep pace with price rises. By the seventeenth and early eighteenth centuries, the ratio of available labour (population) to available land was sufficiently unfavourable for it to lead to the political and economic doctrines of Hobbes and Malthus. Remembering that at that time Europe was racked by major famines on an average of once every decade and a half, it is not surprising that to Hobbes the question was not how to distribute resources fairly – there was not enough to go round in any case – but how to keep society from falling apart under these sordid circumstances, how to prevent the war of all against all. Only a strong ruler could maintain the king's peace. Malthus, writing in the late-eighteenth century, seeing some improvement, accepted that food supplies could grow, but only in linear fashion. Population, on the other hand, grew exponentially. Hence the inevitability of famines and plagues. Ironically, at the time of Malthus' writing, Western Europe had stopped submitting to periodic famines of any great magnitude (the Irish potato famine of the mid-nineteenth century was the exception). The shortage of land emerging in the sixteenth century, and its pre-eminence over the next two or three centuries, gave rise to the analysis of the physiocrats who considered that only land produced wealth – a concept becoming less relevant by the latter half of the eighteenth century as two things were happening: the acreage had been expanding within Europe by clearing woodland in the north and east, and the draining of polders and fens in the west; and European agricultural production was further extended by expanding into the Caribbean and North America. At the same time, improvements in animal husbandry and farming were greatly increasing the productivity of existing land, which was also being cleared of excess labour.

Capital, the third of the triumvirate of land, labour and capital, appears not to have been the limiting factor for most of the eighteenth century. However, as the Industrial Revolution proceeded, land and its ownership became less important, while capital for investing in machines became limiting. First economic, then political, power shifted from the landed aristocrats to the capitalists.

In the 1970s the limiting factor for many industrial and some post-industrial countries was energy (in the form of gas and oil). The ownership of oil and gas had become not only of enormous economic significance but, associated with it, of political power.

In post-industrial economies the limiting factors tend not to be land, labour or capital. The limiting factor in modern productive systems is information (which among other things will either find more oil and gas, find ways of using less, or find alternatives for them). Hence it is the information producers to whom economic and political power accrues.

It is with this theoretical background that it becomes possible to understand why, over the past few centuries, the major economic preoccupation of society has shifted, first from agriculture to manufacturing, and then to information.

A SERVICE ECONOMY

The manufacturing sector has slipped and will continue to slip, both in terms of its share in the gross national product and, in particular, as an employer. Having said that, we should also recognise that a 'post-industrial economy' does not mean an economy in which industry is not important, any more than an industrial economy is one which does not have a sound agricultural base. The recent shift from manufacturing industries to services is parallel to the shift which occurred two centuries ago from agriculture to manufacturing. Just as the pre-eminence of manufacturing industry during the nineteenth century was accompanied by a marked increase in productivity in the agricultural sector, so today do we see the shift to service industries accompanied by a marked increase in productivity in the manufacturing industries. A post-industrial economy is one in which both the number of people employed in manufacturing and the proportion of the gross national product going to manufacturing industries have taken second place to the service sector, a service sector made up of information, not domestic,

operatives. An analysis of the shifting employment pattern suggests that within thirty years it will take no more than 10 per
cent of the labour force to produce all of society's material needs.
That is, all the food, clothing, textiles, furniture, appliances,
automobiles, housing, etc. needed would require no more than
10 per cent of the labour force.

Even the vital 10 per cent in manufacturing will become
more and more involved with handling complex information.
Just as the American farmer at the beginning of the 1980s was
able to produce enough food to feed an average of about sixty
people because he is able to take full advantage of modern
technology and business organisation procedures, so will the
future worker of advanced, automated and robotised factories
be able to design and maintain such systems.

The modern profitable industries, those industries which
expand even during recession, included in the late 1970s
pharmaceuticals, specialised electronics, telecommunications,
computers, new forms of oil and mineral extraction, petrochemicals and agribusiness. In addition the vast improvements
in transportation and communications allow production and
marketing to be properly organised.

The shift to the service sector in post-industrial economics has
centred on knowledge-related services; that is business-related
and professional services. It is important to contrast this post-
industrial service sector with the pre-industrial one which consisted principally of household servants and certain categories
of unskilled retailing staff. This pre-industrial service sector
added relatively little to the productive capacity of the society
and represented more of a consumption item. This pre-industrial sector also included relatively few information operatives,
although agrarian societies did have some(scribes, actors and
priests). As such, this non-information service sector represented
a significant part of the labour force in agrarian, and even
industrial, societies. In post-industrial society it has either virtually disappeared (such as domestic servants) or will rapidly
disappear (petrol pump attendants, shop assistants). In a post-
industrial economy most workers will be people who spend most

of their time manipulating information and getting things started, or alternatively people working with people as in education, health and other caring activities.

Classical economic doctrines two hundred years ago believed that only land produced wealth. Manufacturing, although desirable, merely reworked materials which had come from (or under) the land. There is still a general feeling that today only manufacturing produces real wealth, that the service sector is a kind of reworking, or a supply of useful, but not wealth-generating, services for the primary and manufacturing sectors of the economy – that is, some sort of parasite living off the manufacturing sector. These concepts do not explain why there is such a massive growth in this sector. In Britain, for example, gross trading profits in the service sector have exceeded those in the manufacturing sector since the early 1970s.

THE RISE OF THE INFORMATION OPERATIVE

Classical doctrines cannot explain the profound shift in employment which has affected all the technologically advanced economies. Only by understanding the concept of the information economy does it become comprehensible how, over the last few centuries, there has been a shift in the labour force from farm operatives, to machine operatives, to information operatives.

A CREDIT-BASED ECONOMY

Post-industrial economies are credit-based. Business deals result in the transfer of credit information rather than of actual gold or money. In most post-industrial economies the majority of people are paid by cheque, and the bulk of personal expenditures involves payment by cheque, credit card or standing bank orders. Governments too not only finance budgets on credit, but they hold only a very small proportion of their reserve assets in gold.

The use of 'plastic money' in the form of credit cards has been growing steadily. One of the most successful of these is Visa, a name which appeared only in 1977. By 1980 Visa cards were used to purchase goods worth \$US47.5 billion around the world. The group claims 90 million card holders served by more than 3 million retailers and other businesses. Plastic money will soon be augmented by electronic money, while in the US the technology has developed to a point where home-operated, two-way television banking becomes possible. Note that, in general, all these systems are an extension of the personal cheque which is, after all, merely a piece of paper on which is written the information for transferring credit from one account to another.

The Bank for International Settlements in Switzerland is perhaps the ultimate in transactions involving credit information. Its balance sheet exceeds \$50 billion, including over 200 tonnes of gold. It is housed in an opulent modern building in Basle. Yet it has no vault of its own! Instead it uses the services of the Swiss National Bank, the Bank of England and the New York Federal Reserve Bank. The history of this bank also emphasises the rapid rise in transactions across national boundaries (transnational interactions). Formed in the 1930s to service transnational business deals involving Britain, France, Germany, Belgium and Italy, its membership has grown to twenty-nine countries. The bank's operations are not limited to member states. Virtually every national central bank in the world now holds money with the Bank for International Settlements, and so do the International Monetary Fund and two supranational Comecon banks representing the socialist bloc.

THE ECONOMY IS TRANSNATIONAL, NOT NATIONAL

Productive processes are no longer confined to a single nation but rather have become transnational. This may be illustrated by comparing the production of a high-technology item of the industrial era – a steam locomotive – with a high technology product of the post-industrial era – a jet airliner.

Leeds, in the north of England, was a centre for manufacturing steam locomotives. The raw materials, coal and iron, and their product, steel, all came from the local area. As a result the wheels, the driveshafts, the axles, the pistons, the cylinders, the boilers, the tubes and the chassis were all made locally. The farthest a manufacturer might have gone was to Derby to obtain some specialised gauges or valves, or some specialised steel from Sheffield. The entire complex piece of machinery was made in a limited region and then the completed product might be exported to India or some other country.

The process of building an aeroplane today is a truly international enterprise. The airliner is made up of thousands of components made in a dozen countries. The fuselage might be built in the United States, the engines made by Rolls-Royce in Britain, the fuel injection system manufactured in a third country, the electronic and computerised systems may well come from several others, and so on. Even the basic fuselage may have a global history: the aluminium might be mined in the Caribbean, shipped to the southern United States for crude preliminary refining, transported across the Atlantic to Ghana in Africa where the dam across the Volta river was designed to provide cheap electricity for aluminium smelting, the purified aluminium might then be transported to the British Isles and cast into bars, and, if the price is right, to be transported yet once again across the Atlantic to the United States to build aeroplanes.

Something much less exotic than a jet airliner, the family car, also shows this trend towards transnationalising production. General Motors' 'J car' will be produced in eight different countries from interchangeable parts produced around the world. The engines will be made in Brazil or Australia, the diesel engines in Japan, as will the transaxles and manual transmissions, while automatic transmissions will be manufactured in the US. With some engineering modifications it would be possible to put together a 'world' car whose front end was made by Opel in Germany, its rear end by Holden in Australia, its suspension by GM in North America, its transmission by Isuzo in Japan, and its engine in Brazil (*Financial Times*, 26 August 1981).

The transnationalisation of production can be seen in the trade figures of a country like Britain. At the end of World War II about half of Britain's trade was with her Commonwealth partners. The traditional trading pattern consisted of bringing raw materials into the country and sending manufactured goods back out. Within a quarter of a century that trade had shifted so that now half of the trade went to Britain's EEC partners, while the Commonwealth trade comprised less than a quarter. The expansion of this trade with the EEC involved increasingly the exchange of high-technology products. For some of the smaller European countries, external trade, by the mid-1970s, amounted to about half of their gross national products.

One of the major causes of the transnationalisation of production has been the development of cheap transport and the creation of highly efficient communication systems. Transport costs usually involve only a few per cent of the final price. This has encouraged the shift of labour-intensive industries to Third World countries where labour costs are still cheap, sometimes causing serious dislocations in the West as the more mature industries, such as textiles and steel, moved away from the industrialised countries. It meant that a larger volume of goods could be produced more cheaply. This process contributed to the overall rising standard of living in all parts of the globe, whilst at the same time providing a significant number of jobs in the Third World. The move has been so successful that certain countries, including Taiwan, Korea and Singapore, are leaving the developing country status and moving into developed countries' status, or will do so, probably within a decade.

INSTITUTIONAL ECONOMY RATHER THAN A FREE MARKET

Three powerful factors, the large corporation, the government and the trade unions, dominate the post-industrial economic scene. Large corporations control their economic environment by monopolising certain corners of the market, by fixing the price of their supplies or their product, by putting pressure on government bureaucracies and by public relations campaigns. The government has influence as the largest employer and the largest accumulator of capital and expenditures, directly or indirectly. In almost all the post-industrial countries, public expenditures in some years begin to approach half of the net national income (NNI) and, in a few, come close to two-thirds. Trade unions are able to maintain high wage levels even in times of recession and have pressured most governments to pass minimum wage legislation and other laws relating to working conditions.

Part of the success of the Japanese economy is probably attributable to the fact that its industrial economy has always been more institutionalised than its western counterparts, and that institutions, that is, government, business enterprises and trade unions, have always been much better integrated. This reflects, in part, historical traditions. It also reflects superior education levels.

In addition to the three major factors, the consumer too is becoming increasingly organised. Here both the government and the mass media have become the consumer's major allies, uncovering wrong-doing and providing protective legislation.

It seems probable, however, that this domination by the major factors will decline as we move deeper into the information economy. Advances in technology will allow both the production of goods and the ability to provide services, particularly information services, to decentralise.

UNPRECEDENTED AFFLUENCE

Three hundred years ago serious malnutrition was commonplace as Western Europe was wracked by major famines. A hundred years ago, during industrialisation, major famines had been eliminated, but cases of serious malnutrition were still relatively common. Today, cases of malnutrition in the West make headlines. By any criterion, the material well-being of the average individual has increased enormously. Meat appeared once a week (on Sundays) for most people in the last century, and it was not that long ago when oranges were a luxury. Communally, when we worry about food today in the West, it relates to the 'problem' of surpluses – butter mountains and wine lakes. Gone are the days of being able to recognise 'a gentleman' a hundred yards away because only the rich could afford to dress properly. Virtually every home has indoor plumbing, a television set and other appliances, and most families own a motor car.

There is an enormous improvement as a result of public service expenditures in areas such as health, fire and police protection, education, public transport, communications and pensions.

There are inequities and there is considerable room for improvement. Nevertheless, both those at the bottom end of the socio-economic scale and those in the middle are immeasurably better off than either their industrial progenitors, or those in countries which have not yet passed into the post-industrial economy.

CHANGES ARE ACCELERATING

The more that is known, the easier it is to learn still more. The more that has been invented, the easier it is to invent still more. This is why the pace of change accelerates. Although there are some constraints in time and finances, by and large advances in science and technology fuel further advances. Ninety per cent of all the scientists the world has ever known were alive and working in the 1970s. Scientific literature doubles at least every decade. No wonder that whole new industries appear with remarkable speed, like electronic calculators, while others, such as mechanical calculators – well established for many decades – evaporate equally rapidly.

'Market pull' is being displaced by 'technology push'. That is, there has been a shift from empirical knowledge (often derived from developing technology) leading science to theoretical science shaping technology. Advances in chemistry lead to the synthesis of new compounds in search of a use. Solid-state physics sets the stage for the transistor which then evolves into the micro-processor. The 'miracle chip' looks for new markets. In 1971 the first pocket calculator, costing $240, appeared in the US. Before the end of the decade pocket calculators jumped across the Atlantic so that in Britain on average each household possessed one. Who ever thought of owning a pocket calculator in 1970? What else is happening in micro-electronics? in photo-voltaics? lasers? holography? biomedical technology?

Managers – at least the competent ones – become increasingly nervous as they survey the technology scene. The ignorant ones usually perceive a technological threat to their operations only as it steamrollers over them. The accelerating pace of technological development brings with it not only rapid changes in the economy but, as a consequence, in society as a whole. It leads to a form of cultural disorientation frequently manifesting itself as the re-emergence of orthodox fundamentalist religions, cults and political parties. Coupled to the dislocation caused by a marked increase in unemployment, cultural disorientation may prove to be the most dangerous and unpredictable of the problems emerging in the closing decades of the twentieth century. We have already seen it happen in Moslem countries in which the pace of change appeared intolerable to a sufficient number to have produced an ayatollah, an attempted armed take-over in Mecca by fundamentalists, or the assassination of Egypt's President Sadat.

A PROFILE OF THE POST-INDUSTRIAL ECONOMY (SUMMARY)

The technologically advanced sector of global society has moved into a post-industrial economy whose characteristics may be listed as follows:

(1) It is primarily a service economy rather than a manufacturing one, with the knowledge industry predominating.

(2) As a reflection of (1), the labour force is no longer dominated by people who work with machines (machine operatives), but by information operatives.

(3) It is a credit-based economy characterised by a flow of credit information rather than by cash transactions.

(4) It is primarily transnational rather than national. There has been a great expansion of trade. In particular, the production of manufactured goods requires not only raw materials from other countries, but an increasing number of manufactured components as well. As such, the productive processes themselves have become transnationalised.

(5) It is primarily an institutional rather than a free market economy. There have emerged three major economic institutions: the government, the large corporations and the trade unions, whose combined impact on the economy exceeds that of the individual, the household or the small firm. These major institutions, in particular the government, engage increasingly in planning the economy.

(6) The post-industrial economy is characterised by unprecedented affluence both at the private level and in the public sector.

(7) Changes are taking place at an exponential rate rather than linearly.

3 Information operatives – how they fit in

'In the work of cutlers and locksmiths ... and in all those goods which are commonly known by the name of Birmingham and Sheffield ware .... It has ... been sufficient to astonish the workmen of every other part of Europe, who in many cases acknowledge that they can produce no work of equal goodness for double, or even for triple the price. There are perhaps no manufactures in which the division of labour can be carried further, or in which the machinery employed admits of a greater variety of improvements ...'
Adam Smith, Book One, Chapter XI.

Those 'improvements' of which Adam Smith speaks reflected both the learned skills of the cutlers and locksmiths, and the ingenuity and know-how embodied in the design of the machinery. Wealth has always at least partially depended on knowledge. As early as the late eighteenth century, it was already becoming apparent to theorists like Adam Smith that trade introduced the ideas which created the best manufacturing in a city, and trade and advanced manufacturing together provided the innovations and capital to improve local agriculture. The process has continued until, in the post-industrial economy, knowledge has displaced the traditional land, labour and capital as the most important single input into modern productive systems. In fact, modern productive systems have become so complex that most of people's efforts go into getting things organised. This accounts for the rise of the information operatives as the dominant form of labour.

The displacement of land by knowledge is exemplified by skyscrapers, and by the release of millions of acres devoted to growing oats and other horse feeds as tractors came to displace horses. The development of marine agriculture or cattle feed from single-cell protein will repeat this process. There is still a need for land in some of these examples but no farmland is required to 'feed' tractors (unlike horses). Knowledge may also 'create' new land, by sea or desert reclamations.

Labour is displaced by knowledge every time we raise productivity through mechanisation, automation or better organisation.

Knowledge can displace capital by decreasing the cost of production, hence the amount of capital required. The most dramatic example of this is the reduction in the cost of computers. In 1960 the simplest functional circuit needed two transistors and five other components. By 1978 twenty thousand functions could be placed on a single silicon chip. This growth in circuit density drove down the cost of an electronic function by a thousandfold – from ten dollars in 1960 to below one cent by 1978. The amount of capital required per unit of computer power declined dramatically both for the producer and for the consumer.

Another way for knowledge to displace capital is the increasing tendency to substitute credit information for money. Money itself exists only by virtue of the information it contains. Gold or silver, when used as money, contain the tacit agreement as to what it is worth. The agreed value of paper money has the backing of the state, although the value placed on its money by some states does not coincide with the value others place on it – hence the appearance of currency restrictions and black markets. If money contains information then it is possible to create capital by changing the information patterns, for example by requiring lower gold reserves to cover the money in circulation. J. K. Galbraith writes amusingly about the origin of modern banking in Amsterdam in the seventeenth century. Deposits created in the Amsterdam banks could be lent out. Banks then got interest while borrowers had credit (capital) to be spent, and depositors had available to them credit (capital) which they could also spend. Thus the same amount of money could just about double as credit capital – as long as all the creditors and depositors did not rush on the bank at the same time.

INFORMATION CREATES WEALTH

Information can create wealth by being sold directly. Information sales may involve a patent, copyright or licence. The famous E. Cuncliffe Lister, who was renowned for making the Queen's velvet and whose mill in Bradford began to mass-produce silks, velvets and plushes in the mid-nineteenth century, made a good deal of his money on textile machinery patents and licencing arrangements. Owning a good patent can be worth more than owning a whole factory.

Adam Smith actually calculated how much wealth those most famous information operatives of ancient times, the Greek philosophers, managed to accrue:

> Isocrates himself demanded ten minae, or thirty-three pounds six shillings and eight pence, from each scholar. When he taught at Athens, he is said to have had a hundred scholars ... He must have made, therefore, by each course of lectures, a thousand minae, or £3,333 6s. 8d. A thousand minae ... it is said by Plutarch ... to have been his ... price for teaching. Many other eminent teachers in those times appear to have acquired great fortunes. Gorgias made a present to the temple of Delphi of his own statue in solid gold ... Plato ... is said to have lived with a good deal of magnificence. Aristotle, after having been the tutor to Alexander, the most magnificently rewarded ... both by him and his father Philip, thought it worthwhile ... to return to Athens, in order to resume the teaching of his school. (Adam Smith, pp. S237–238.)

Today the most important information operatives are managers who possess organisational expertise. They are among the most highly salaried members of the post-industrial economy. They create new wealth by coupling information to existing organisations or productive systems, thereby reducing the costs of production or by creating new products or services. They must weld into a viable organisation not only machine operatives (sometimes also farm operatives) but a whole host of other information operatives who, in a large firm, may include those involved with accounting, finance, cash flows, taxes, contracts, personnel, industrial relations, public relations, community relations, recruitment, planning, forecasting, research, product development, new products, design, education and training, sources of supply, energy conservation, plant maintenance, repairs, engineering, office management, advertising, marketing, sales networks, communications, competitors and company policy. Each of these activities may involve managers who supervise further information operatives, such as draftsmen, technical salesmen and filing clerks. It is this web of information and information operatives which determines the success (wealth creation ability) or failure of the product. A significant failure in any of the departments listed above could cause a collapse of the whole enterprise, although there may be substantial lags between a specific failure and the full impact.

Industries whose information base is at the forefront of human knowledge are those which can move upstream technologically, ahead of others, and whose profits continue even when there is a recession. Usually they involve entirely new products which have created new markets for themselves (e.g. antibiotics, pocket calculators) or they have improved their productivity so effectively as to leave competitors behind. These enterprises represent an investment of capital and an enormous investment in knowledge.

Texas Instruments is a classic example: during the recession years of the mid-1970s it expanded from a $1 billion sales per year industry in 1973 to a $2 billion industry by 1977. Part of its success related to the decision to move into the hand-held calculator technology in the early 1970s when that market hardly existed. The company continued to build up its leadership in fast-moving high-technology semi-conductors, calculators and digital watches. Both the research budgets and capital expenditures for expanded and improved production have been substantial – totalling about $240 million for research, and about $700 million capital expenditure during the 1975–8 period.

It is not only individual firms for whom the use of advancing knowledge can be crucial to overcoming general economic adversities, it can be true for entire countries. Japan and Switzerland have a shortage of land and a dearth of mineral resources, yet both are economic powers. If their power and wealth is not based on an indigenous physical resource, what is it based on? Clearly on their human resources – the skill, education and discipline of their workforce. It is noteworthy that both Japan and Switzerland have an extraordinarily high number of patents granted on a *per capita* basis. By 1973 Japan led the world in the number of patents granted, ahead of the USSR, the USA and the nine countries of the EEC put together.

Technological know-how is often hidden under the rubric of 'economies of scale'. Texas Instruments understands fully the value of the 'learning curve' which involves applying new know-how. Contrast their view with the more classical concepts expressed by the chairman of the Electricity Council in a 1978 article entitled 'Economies of Scale in Electricity Generation and Transmission Since 1945'. The article briefly reviews the advances in technology of steam engines since 1727. It then contrasts the first central power stations erected in the early 1890s with the large power plants erected in the late 1970s. The capital cost dropped from £2,500 per kW to one-tenth that figure.

The improvements in performance reflected the use of larger turbo-alternators, larger machinery and higher steam conditions. All of these represent technological know-how: they are part of the learning curve. Decreasing costs of production and decreasing capital requirements always require an increase in effective information – either technological or organisational.

EDUCATED PEOPLE CREATE WEALTH

'A man educated at the expense of much labour and time ... may be compared to one of those expensive machines.' So wrote Adam Smith two centuries ago. The matter is analogous to adding value to material by applying labour. That is, just as weaving wool into cloth adds value to that wool, so does education add value to a person.

At the end of the 1940s British shipyards built about half of the world's ships. At the end of the 1960s the Japanese did.

From personal reports one gathers the impression that the education levels of the two countries were very different. There was virtually no formal higher education among British managers, an occasional 'Higher National Diploma' – the men had come up from practical experience. The yard workers likewise had little in the way of general skills training. Again, the emphasis was on practical experience. In contrast, the Japanese had a highly trained and skilled workforce. It was a rare manager who had no higher education and most had advanced engineering degrees. Question: with new technology and new concepts developing all the time, who was more likely to incorporate new ideas and new technology, the British manager or the Japanese? Is it any wonder that the Japanese rapidly incorporated new design features into their ships and improved their production methods? Japanese ships were built at less cost, were of better quality and were delivered on time... By the end of the 1970s British shipbuilders were losing tens of millions of pounds annually and survived only at taxpayers' expense.

Japanese shipbuilding is itself, however, not immune from competition. By the early 1980s it was probably true to say that the newest, the biggest and the best in shipyards had developed in South Korea. Hyundai's sprawling Mipo Bay complex at Ulsan had become either the world's biggest or close to it. In 1980 it took first place in tonnage completed, second place in tonnage launched. In 1981 it took first place in both, completing over 1.3 million tons (dwt) and launching over 1.6 million. In addition it developed an enormous business in ship repairing. Daewoo's newly opened yard at Okpo Bay has been described as a 'space age' complex with a 'Grand Canyon' of a building dock, able (should anyone so desire) to build a one-million ton ship. The dock is serviced by the world's largest crane which can lift a 900-ton section almost thirty storeys. In addition to the two giants, South Korea has a number of smaller, but still sizeable, yards such as Korea Shipbuilding and Engineering, Samsung, Dae-Dong, Dae-Sun, Inchon, Korea Tacoma and Dong Hae. Even though the world shipbuilding trade was in a serious recession in the early 1980s, the Korean yards' order books were full. This success reflects not merely the sheer size of investment in steel and concrete – not even the advanced state of the technology employed. It must also be attributed to the quality of the human capital involved. Hong In-Kie, president of Daewoo Shipbuilding, is quoted as saying: 'Our manpower is our great resource ... we are always trying to improve the minds of the workers – and that includes myself. Seven of my top colleagues have a PhD...' Similarly, the senior executive managing director of Samsung, American-educated K. U. Chee, has stated: 'We feel education is very important here, and all the workers have fifteen minutes of English lessons every day.'

An educated workforce learns how to exploit new technology; an ignorant one becomes its victim.

The value of human capital in shipbuilding is illustrated by the case of William Doxford & Sons. At one point in the 1930s 90 per cent of the world's marine diesel engines were either being built or designed by Doxford. Even in the late 1940s Doxford remained the world leader, particularly with its famous 'Cathedral' engine. In November 1952 the chairman's statement referred to the engine as '... the foremost marine oil engine of the day'. It was taller than a three-storey house. In the late 1940s and 1950s Doxford was building about fifty or sixty engines a year, making handsome profits. However, competition was appearing on the horizon, in particular from the Swiss firm Sulzer and a Danish firm, Burmeister and Wain. By the early 1960s Doxford's share of the world market (as horse-power installed) had declined to under 2 per cent. It never recovered. During the 1970s it lost money virtually every year – in 1978, £4.5 million. By 1979 it was decided to close down the operation except for making spare parts for existing Doxford engines. Incidentally, by 1979, Sulzer was building or designing about half of the world's slow-speed diesel engines while Burmeister and Wain were doing about a quarter.

In the 1930s the Doxford engine was the most advanced in the world, but the credit goes to a Swiss, Otto Keller, who was Doxford's technical director. Keller died in 1942. His successor

lacked the necessary technological flair. Doxford coasted on
Keller's success for some time. When more power was needed,
it simply increased the size of the engine, until crankshaft problems led to breakdowns. In 1958 Doxford attempted to re-
establish its reputation as a world leader. It bought in new
engineering skills and developed turbo-charged engines and
improved its earlier, opposed-piston engines (first pioneered by
Otto Keller). Matters began to improve. However, the company began to make mistakes. It is clear that whoever made the
final decisions did not understand the market (and probably
not the technology either). Successful judgements are based on
having available all the relevant information on the one hand
and sophisticated individuals who know how to interpret that
information on the other. Ignorance breeds failure. Practical
experience helps, but a broad theoretical understanding becomes increasingly important in a technological, rapidly moving information society. A feature in successful industrial innovation is the presence of an outstanding person in a position of
authority. Such a 'top person' (a manager, managing director,
technical director or chairman) might be the one who identifies
a useful area to explore initially or who, alternatively, if
presented with a good idea can generate the enthusiasm and
provide the resources required for the successful conclusion of a
project. Although the personal qualities of such a top person
play an important role, judgements can be no better than the
information available, and the ability to interpret that information intelligently and imaginatively.

Opportunity favours trained minds, both of management
and workforce. A study by the National Institute of Economic
and Social Research concluded that the industry in Britain was
'technologically backward'. The study points out that about
half of the machine tool industrial labour force in both Britain
and West Germany is classed as 'skilled'. Yet those so classified
in Britain have not been required to attend any courses or pass
any practical or theoretical tests. Furthermore, in contrast to
Germany, a bigger pay packet does not depend on the achieve-
ment of any certified standard.

In August 1980 the headline 'UK training is West's worst' appeared (*Observer*, 3 August 1980). Based on a report to the Manpower Services Commission, it pointed out that up to 44 per cent of young people go into the labour market with no training at all. Fourteen per cent win an apprenticeship, 10 per cent enter full-time vocational training. Less than a third go on to full-time higher education. In West Germany two-thirds of the men and half of the women on the labour market have vocational qualifications through practical and theoretical testing, and theirs is not an isolated case.

This is also true for Third World farmers (FT 18 August 1980). Farmers with four years of primary education produce about 13 per cent more than those without education. Between 1950 and 1975 adult literacy in middle-income developing countries rose from 48 to 71 per cent. In low-income countries it rose from 22 to 38 per cent. The fastest developing countries had above average literacy rates. Literacy contributes to increased output per worker and increased investment.

Educating girls may be one of the best investments a country can make in future growth. Even if girls never enter the labour force, it is mothers rather than fathers whose influences are crucial for children. In addition, educated women marry later and are more likely to know about family planning. In Brazil, families were better fed the higher the mother's education.

A fit workforce is more energetic and more adaptable; it is more likely to innovate and accept innovation. The pronounced increases in yield per acre of wheat in England, and rice in Japan late in the nineteenth century, correlate with the introduction of mass education. The continuing increases in productivity correlate with continuing improvements in both education and mass communication.

Today American farmers are perhaps the most productive in the world. They work from an enormous information base which has accumulated over centuries. To utilise it properly they must know about fertilisers and soil conditions, hybrid seeds and crop rotation, insecticides and weed killers, how to select a tractor, drive a combine harvester, maintain farm machinery, haggle with commodity speculators who will pay for a crop before it is planted, keep records and accounts, organise cooperatives to build storage silos, follow the latest technological developments, etc. etc. If they deal with livestock, they will know about hybrid cattle and antibiotics, and may run a computer to optimise feeding routines. If they grow crops, no longer do they plant one crop year after year as their fathers did before. It's wheat one year, maize the next and soyabeans the year after that, depending on the price they can get from a food processing firm or the grain speculator whose information reveals what commodities are likely to be in short supply next year. American farmers of today usually have a university degree and know how to be a part-time cultivator, mechanic, veterinarian or plant pathologist, soil chemist, computer operator, accountant and manager. By the late 1970s the average world farmer fed five people, while the average Western European farmer fed twenty. The average American farmer fed close to sixty.

Training provides skills. Education provides meta-skills. Meta-skills are a sort of superskill which allow one to acquire other skills more easily. American farmers have not only skills which they learned on the farm, or from elementary education, but their higher education gave them meta-skills. Among the various metaskills must rank highly the knowledge about to whom to go for help, and when – accountants, lawyers, veterinarians, local county agents, university plant pathology departments, technical salesmen, meteorologists and garage mechanics. Meta-skills allow one to obtain needed information and assimilate it readily even though the information is outside one's own expertise. The more educated one becomes, the more versatile one becomes. (This is a somewhat different concept of education from the prevailing one which confuses advanced university training, whether in engineering or the classics, with education.)

INFORMATION OPERATIVES

Given the importance of human capital, and given the fact that information has become the most important input into modern

production systems, it becomes easy to see why the post-industrial labour force is dominated by information operatives.

Modern productive systems involve a complex interaction of
land, labour, capital, machinery, energy and material inputs
coupled to equally complex transport, communication and distribution systems. To get these various facets properly organised
requires a host of organisation operatives – managers. They
represent one kind of information operatives. Another kind is
involved with the transmission of information – secretaries,
telephone operators, postal workers, journalists and others
working in the mass media, educators of all sorts, technical
salesmen. A third category is involved with information storage
and retrieval – filing clerks, librarians, computer programmers.
A relatively small number is involved in creating new information, or patterns of information – scientists, artists, statisticians,
architects, designers. A fifth category applies information in
order to solve specific problems – lawyers, doctors, counsellors,
accountants. Last, there is a large group of information operatives who are not normally considered part of the labour force
(but historically used to be) – people who make their living
receiving information – students.

Over twenty years ago the economist Fritz Machlup, in his
book *The Production and Distribution of Knowledge in the United States*,
pointed to the gradual, but distinct, shift in unemployment
patterns (at least since 1900) with a rapid trend by mid-cen-
tury which shifted manual labour and manual skills to information labour and brainpower. It was Machlup who defined
the 'knowledge industry' and whose pioneering study has influenced much of the thinking in this book. During the 1950s the
US labour force as a whole increased by 17 per cent. According
to Machlup, the increase in all knowledge-producing occupations was 30 per cent. The technical/professional group grew by
43 per cent. This reflects a long-term trend: the share of
knowledge-producing occupations in the total labour force tri-
pled during the first six decades of this century. Within this
increase, Machlup points to a trend within a trend, a succession
of occupations: first clerical, then administrative and manager-

ial, finally technical and professional. 'Thus, the changing employment pattern indicates a continuing movement from manual to mental and from less to more highly trained labour.'

Educated and skilled labour tends to be more productive. Hence there is a continuous selective pressure favouring the educated and skilled, and discriminating against the uninformed and unskilled. The worker with the shovel is displaced by the bulldozer driver, while the filing clerk is displaced by the computer programmer. In some instances, a trade or profession is deskilled as a result of advances in technology or technique. When this happens, it is now only a matter of time before such deskilled jobs become eliminated altogether. The history of the textile trade is a case in point.

Daniel Bell has provided further data on the rise of the information operatives in the US. Between 1947 and 1964 the employment of professional and technical workers more than doubled, rising by half again by 1975. By the mid-1970s about 15 per cent of the labour force could be classed as professional/ technical. Teachers make up the largest group of this class, engineers are second, engineering and science technicians a third. Growth for the crucial fourth group, scientists, has been remarkable: whereas the growth of the total workforce increased by 50 per cent between 1930 and 1965, advanced engineers increased by 370 per cent, and scientists by 930 per cent.

In the UK, the rise of information employment has been spectacular both in absolute terms and as a percentage of total employment. It provided 2.2 million new jobs during the 1951-71 period. In addition, during this twenty-year period, the number of persons aged 15 + in full-time education rose from 556 thousand in 1951 to 994 thousand in 1961, then jumped to 1.785 million by 1971. When full-time 'students' are included in the category of information operatives, the percentage of the UK labour force in information employment rose from about 21 per cent in 1951 to 26 per cent in 1961 and 33 per cent in 1971.

The rise of the information operative may be demonstrated in the long-term trends in higher education. Professor E. G.

Edwards, past vice-chancellor of Bradford University, in a study conducted with I. J. Roberts has shown that in most countries of western Europe there started, in 1860, a steady doubling of students in higher education. Over the next century, student enrollment expanded nearly sixteen times with a remarkable uniform trend which deviated only temporarily as a result of the two great European wars. Following this growth, as society moved into the communicative era, a new trend appeared over the 1955–70 period, showing a substantially faster increase (from doubling every twenty-five years to doubling in only nine years). After 1970 there are fluctuations and a retrenchment. Presumably this will prove to be temporary. The recession in education probably reflects the economic uncertainties and social confusion resulting from the transition to a post-industrial, information economy. The disillusion with education reflects, in part, the inability of the education system to adapt to the changing requirements of the new economy.

In the US the university population has doubled every twenty years since 1879. Between 1960 and 1970 the number of university students doubled, partly because of the population bulge. Nevertheless, the major reason is what Daniel Bell calls the 'democratisation of higher education'. Bell points out that in the US, just as in the 1920s there was a conscious public decision to make secondary education available to all, so did a post-war consensus emerge to provide at least some form of higher education to all youth.

THE KNOWLEDGE INDUSTRY

Universities provide employment and improve human capital, and produce new ideas and new industries. This becomes increasingly important as advances in technology become less dependent on individual trial-and-error inventors, and more dependent on theoretical knowledge. In the early industrial era technology preceded science; the reverse is true today.

Basic research in solid-state physics preceded and led to the transistor. The location of the semi-conductor industry in the early 1950s clustered along Route 128 in Boston. Many of the founders of the new companies were graduates of the Massachusetts Institute of Technology and Harvard who frequently either recruited other staff from local universities or consulted with university experts. Local Boston brainpower was not only limited to technical know-how, but also to business acumen. In their study Braun and MacDonald found that the availability of risk capital was equally crucial in the rise of the early semiconductor industry in the Boston area. Again the question: which bank managers or other investors are more likely to provide such capital – technical ignoramuses, or individuals sufficiently educated to get 'a feel' for the technological opportunities?

Universities generate new industries if the climate is right, such as Silicon Valley and the northern California University complex, and Wood, who started Oxford Instruments by making magnets in his own house. Even a university as recently established as the University of Bradford has already given rise to about a dozen small businesses, including making new scientific instruments, consultancies, a publishing firm and a company producing educational software for computers.

'Education' is the largest of the knowledge industries, according to Fritz Machlup. He includes not only formal educational institutions but considers also education in the home, in the church and in the armed services. Another important component of the knowledge industry, largely financed (as in education) by government funds is 'research and development'.

The third major component of the knowledge industry covers the 'media of communication' – printing, publishing, books, periodicals, newspapers, theatre and film, radio and television, telephone and telegraph, the postal service, and so forth. A fourth division of the knowledge industry consists of 'information machines' such as typewriters, computers, automatic control systems, musical instruments and signalling devices. Last, there exists a sector of the knowledge industry, more difficult to define, which includes a good deal of consultation and advice by specialists, record keeping, data processing and data transmission, specialised sales talk and specialised advice in bringing together potential sellers and buyers. Legal, engineering, architectural, medical, accounting and auditing services are fairly clear-cut. Machlup suggests in conclusion that in 1958 about 29 per cent of the US GNP was spent on knowledge.

The pioneering studies of Machlup and Bell have been updated by a nine-volume joint project of the US National Science Foundation and the Department of Commerce under the direction of Marc Porat. Porat begins by dividing the information sector into two major sub-groups: the 'primary information sector' which includes those firms supplying information goods and services within a market context, and the 'secondary information sector' which includes all the information services produced for internal consumption by government and private, non-information firms. In 1967 the primary information sector accounted for 25 per cent of the US GNP; the secondary sector for an additional 21 per cent: information activity including both market and non-market transactions, accounted for 46 per cent of GNP in 1967. Porat may not be right but how wrong can he be? And if Porat's analysis implies that almost half of the United States GNP was based on information activities in 1967, how much of the country's GNP is tied up in information activities in the early 1980s?

A measure of the growth of the information sector of the economy since Porat's analysis may be ascertained by looking at certain technological indicators. For example, in 1967 there were roughly 15, 000 computer terminals in use in the USA. By 1980 there were probably in excess of two million. Computer terminals may plug into networks of computer data bases which allow one to try to pull together a complete body of available information on any subject. The process of using computers in this manner is called 'on-line searches'. On-line searches hardly existed in the 1960s; in 1970–71 there were between one hundred and two hundred thousand of them; by around 1980 there were at least two million. The world's bibliographic files and numeric data bases used in the on-line searches increased from about 500 in 1976 to about three times that number by 1980.

One of the great problems which needs to be confronted by information economists is the problem of quantification. How do you measure information in economic terms? How do you measure the productivity of an information operative? One can determine fairly easily the percentage of the GNP spent on information, but how do you measure its long-term impact on the economy? Machlup and Porat have helped to define what percentage of the economy is engaged in information activities. Porat's division of the information sector into a primary (market) and secondary (internal consumption) sector is most useful. What has not yet been properly defined is the fruits of that activity. What percentage of annual growth of GNP, or increase in the quality of life (not always the same thing), is attributable to advances in information or education? There is a great need for the best brains of our times to address themselves to this challenge – to create a new branch of economics, information economics.

4 Wealth through knowledge

'As the capital of an individual can be increased only by what he saves from his annual revenue or his annual gains, so the capital of a society, which is the same with that of all the individuals who compose it, can be increased only in the same manner.

'Parsimony, and not industry, is the immediate cause of the increase of capital. Industry, indeed, provides the subject which parsimony accumulates. But whatever industry might acquire, if parsimony did not save and store up, the capital would never be the greater.'

Adam Smith, Book Two, Chapter III.

The wealth of a nation may actually be increased by means other than those described by Adam Smith – military conquest, for one – but more importantly, by the use of technology to transform non-resources into resources. This has induced wealth-creating discontinuities of greater importance to human history than the interminable fighting over inadequate resources. Some societies have grown very rich indeed as a result of technological jumps.

SOME HISTORICAL EXPERIENCES

A thousand years ago, not many people would have guessed that northern Europe would someday gain ascendancy over Mediterranean Europe, the Arabs, the Turks, finally the whole world. However, a thousand years ago the signs were already there. Europe had begun to leave behind its Dark Ages. A poor, backward and barbaric part of the world was beginning to grow and prosper. With prosperity came mercantilism on the one hand, and a population explosion on the other. As Hugh Trevor-Roper has pointed out, by the eleventh century, Europe was bulging at the seams. The excess population had to be siphoned off. The Normans went west. The Swedes and Poles went east. Finally, the Christian gentlemen of Europe were united under one holy banner to go after the people who really had the riches – the Arabs.

What was at the base of this transformation from a poor, backward and militarily weak region into a thriving, vigorous and powerful society? It was the 'Agricultural Revolution' of the ninth and tenth centuries, centred on the deep plough and ancillary technology. To quote from Lynn White's book, *Medieval Technology and Social Change*: 'By the early ninth century all the major interlocking elements of this revolution had been developed: the heavy plough, the open fields, the modern harness, the triennial rotation ...' About a hundred years later there was further support in the form of nailed horseshoes, while earlier, the use of the heavy axe helped clear the land in the first place. The clue here is White's term 'interlocking elements', for it was not any one single invention, but an evolving system, a new way of doing things, using a diversity of technological developments which effected the transformation: unproductive woodlands were transformed into highly productive farmland.

This transformation was limited to Europe's northern plains. As White points out, it is here that the heavy plough was appropriate to the rich soils, where the summer rains favoured a large spring planting. Contrast this with the dry soils of the Mediterranean civilisations, subject to erosion if disturbed too much – as the Romans grieved to discover when their resource base collapsed. As the granaries of North Africa eroded, so did Roman power.

In the Agrarian Era, almost all production related to land. Therefore the technological transformation of woodland to farmland in the ninth and tenth centuries was of such major importance. A similar situation arose in the Netherlands in the late sixteenth century – the draining of the polders. It turned a non-resource, land at the bottom of ponds or the North Sea, into highly productive farmlands. Here the technology centred on the water-pumping windmill. By putting a dyke around the pond, then digging a ditch around the dyke and pumping the water out into the ditch and finally to the sea, some of the most fertile land in the world was uncovered. The polders still yield plentifully today. The 'Golden Age' of the Dutch occurred in the middle of the seventeenth century. Undoubtedly a significant part of that Dutch wealth and splendour can be attributed to those transformed polders.

This technology spread across the North Sea in the sixteenth century. The Norfolk fens began to be drained. Again much of Britain's wealth in the eighteenth century, when according to at least one economic historian, it became the 'granary of Europe', must be attributed to the transformation of huge tracts of relatively unproductive marshlands to highly productive farmland. Those eastern counties, incidentally, are still the backbone of much of Britain's highly successful agriculture.

A boost to development in all fields was a major new development in the knowledge industry – the introduction of printing. Although Johann Gutenberg is frequently credited with the invention of the printing press in the 1440s, the technology had existed for some time in Europe and Asia. Gutenberg perfected certain aspects but it was a technology already so widely diffused that within thirty years there were 236 printing presses in Italy (Venice became a major printing centre), seventy-eight in Germany and sixty-eight elsewhere. By 1500 the number of printing presses in Europe had more than doubled again. During the sixteenth century publishing became distinct from printing. Antwerp, already a major trading centre, also became a centre of book publishing, where the firm of Plantin possessed twenty-two presses and employed up to 160 workmen – a major industrial enterprise for the early sixteenth century. Actually, Plantin received some of its working capital from King Philip II, so that it was an early version of Her Majesty's Stationery Office (HMSO), the Government Printing Office. The same could be said for the Aldine Press in Venice, which was patronised by the Pope, and Estienne the French publisher, subsidised by the French kings. The most important books in terms of size of the editions consisted of books of devotion: Catholic breviaries, or the Hugenot Psalter, which in 1569 involved an edition of 35,000 copies. In the long run, of greater significance were schoolbooks like Erasmus' *Colloquia* for Latin students, or De Villedieu's *Doctrinal* for teaching grammar, textbooks such as Besson's *Theatre of Instruments*, and others written by Ramelli, Veranzio, Branca and Zonca connecting the arts and crafts of the classical period. Even more important were the new works on metallurgy, mining and chemical technology by Biringuccio, Agricola, Ercker and Lohneiss. Unlike their medieval predecessors, the craftsmen of the late sixteenth century were in a position to consult the descriptions and instructions of their colleagues.

MINERAL AND ENERGY RESOURCES

If technology can transform waste lands into highly productive lands, the matter can be even more dramatic in terms of mineral and energy resources. Take oil, for example. The most important single global energy source for much of the twentieth century started off as a nuisance to Pennsylvania farmers – who sent irate letters to local newspapers in the middle of the nineteenth century. By late in the twentieth century the richest countries in the world (on a *per capita* basis) were the oil-rich Arab countries. Kuwait, for example, had become sufficiently affluent to provide free public telephone service, health care and free education through university for all Kuwaiti citizens. It had major investment holdings all over the world. How did Kuwait accumulate all that wealth? By a lot of people putting their savings in building societies? By producing masses of dates for sale to hungry Europeans? By conquest, or by trading slaves? Classical economic doctrines on capital formation would not consider the input of information as the major source of wealth. Yet it was technological and organisational know-how which acted as the limiting factor. The Kuwaiti oil had been there since long before the ancient civilisations developed on those sunny shores. A century ago, if you drilled for anything, it was water, not oil. Only with modern technology did oil become a significant resource, and only with modern technology did it become possible to find it and extract it.

The value of the British pound started to rise fairly steadily in the late 1970s, even though by any number of indicators, Britain's economy seemed to be doing rather poorly. The reason: Britain had acquired a major new resource: oil – in sufficient quantities to meet domestic needs and to export. Britain had become wealthy and the international financial community understood this very well. By 1980-81 the Exchequer was receiving about £2.5 billion in revenues and taxes from the offshore oil industry.

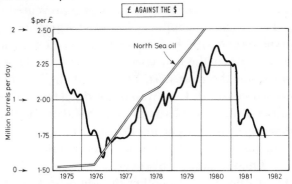

Unfortunately for the British, just as the oil began to flow in significant quantities, the 1970s oil crisis started to recede and the price of oil began to fall – as did the value of the pound. Nevertheless, it was still a boon. Note that North Sea oil had been there since long before the battle of Hastings – but it was a non-resource until expertise developed it into a wealth producer. The information required for finding it, drilling for it, selling it (even though it was quite expensive to produce), transporting it, came from scientists, geologists, engineers, marine specialists, managers, financiers, shippers. That is, it was the human capital which put together the combination of land (under the sea), labour and capital. The key factor at each step was knowledge. Not only the British, but the Norwegians, too, have prospered from the North Sea bonanza, while the Dutch standard of living was enhanced by a comparable development of natural gas.

However, it is not only by discovering and exploiting previously untapped resources that knowledge creates new wealth. A resource may be present, but not properly utilised until sufficient knowledge has become available. An example of this is the coking process for iron making introduced in the early eighteenth century. The British iron industry had been declining steadily since the early seventeenth century. Britain faced an energy crisis at the beginning of the seventeenth century because it had run out of wood. Over a period of centuries much of the countryside, and particularly the wooded hills, had been deforested, then turned over to sheep (which prevented reforestation). The declining supplies of wood became increasingly inadequate to cope with the increase in population, agriculture and industry. Enter the new energy source: coal. That solved the problem for the most part, but not for the iron industry. They needed charcoal. Coal would not do. The iron industry shifted from Britain to Germany and Sweden. Increasingly, Swedish imports were displacing British iron.

In 1709 Abraham Darby, a member of that illustrious Coalbrookdale Quaker family, discovered how to produce coke-smelted cast iron. It took another decade or so to perfect the process. This allowed Darby to make cylinders for Newcomen's steam engine, which became commercially successful about the same time (ca. 1712) but initially had to be made of brass. By 1722 Abraham Darby's firm could cast such cylinders out of its coke-smelted iron and this product became an important part of the firm's trade. In 1763 the Darby firm cast a 7-ton cylinder, $10\frac{1}{2}$ feet long and over 6 feet in diameter. Cast iron was rapidly beginning to replace wood for many engineering components, such as windmill shafts, water wheel shafts and gear wheels, while Abraham Darby III built the iron bridge over the Severn in 1779. One might well ponder the fate of the Industrial Revolution had Abraham Darby not known how to convert coal into iron-smelting coke, or had the knowledge contributed by all the other craftsmen, artisans, engineers and inventors never materialised. The Industrial Revolution created unparalleled amounts of wealth. Without a massive expansion of Europe's information base, it would never have happened.

POTENTIAL FOR THE FUTURE

There exist at least four major technologies which, if properly developed, could make Britain energy-independent even after the oil runs out as well as a net exporter of chemicals and a net exporter of food. They are the conversion of coal to oil, gas and chemicals; developing wave-powered electricity generators; coastal fish-farming; and single-cell protein for livestock feed.

The conversion of coal into oil is a fairly mature technology. In 1951 the South African Coal, Oil and Gas Corporation began constructing its first plant to produce oil from coal. The capital was provided by the state in the form of share capital. By 1955 construction was complete; 'Sasol One' went into operation. In 1974, in response to the oil crisis of late 1973, the South African Minister of Economic Affairs announced the decision to build a second plant. Thus 'Sasol Two' was born. Based on twenty-five years of experience, Sasol Two developed three key operations. The first converts coal into crude gas, the second purifies the gas and the third converts the purified gas into hydrocarbons.

The experience gained has been sufficient for two oil companies each to start building billion-dollar plants in the United States. Other countries such as Belgium and Germany have also been experimenting, while the UK's National Coal Board, combined with the British Gas Corporation, put forth proposals in 1978 to the Coal Industry Tripartite Group for a massive research and development programme for advanced coal extraction and utilisation.

This proposed £122 million programme is designed to test six different processes which would produce (from coal) industrial fuel gas, substitute natural gas, petrol, diesel and transport fuels, chemical feedstocks plus direct electrical power generation. In view of Britain's enormous known coal reserves, including additional sources under the North and Irish Seas, it would be sensible to develop such a program so that as the oil runs out an environmentally acceptable version of coal can take its place.

ENERGY FROM THE SEA

In contrast to the chemicals-from-coal technology, obtaining electricity from ocean waves is still immature. It is technically feasible, but the economics of it are still uncertain. Wave power (not to be confused with tidal power, which should also be developed but which is a relatively mature technology) is one of the most promising sources of electricity based on a renewable energy source. It is a natural for the British Isles, placed as they are on the leeward side of a highly energetic ocean. Waves along the Atlantic coast are among the most energetic in the world. Normally about 6 to 10 feet high, they contain about 40 to 90 kW for every 3 feet of wave front – enough to supply electrical energy for several households if you assume that you could extract and bring on-shore about half that power. With a coast-line exceeding well over 1000 miles, North Atlantic wave power represents a far larger potential for the British Isles than any other renewable energy source.

Although the technology is still embryonic, it has made re-markable strides in the last half decade. Britain is probably the leader, but Japan and the US are also significantly involved, and the International Energy Agency in Paris is sponsoring a joint project between the US, Britain, Ireland, Canada and Japan. There are a large number of devices being tested, in-cluding among others, the Salter duck, the Cockerell raft, the rectifier, the Lancaster flexible bag, the Kaimei and the Masuda buoy. Variants of this last device have been used by the Japanese since 1965 for powering navigational buoys. In 1966 they in-stalled such a system to power the Ashika-Jima lighthouse in Tokyo bay. The system has been highly successful.

It is not yet possible to ascertain which of the many different types of wave-power devices will prove to be economically successful. But that one, or several will become so is highly probable. The question is how soon. That is strictly a function of how much money and other resources are put into the pro-gramme including labour and materials. Developing wave power involves no new theoretical breakthroughs. It is merely a series of engineering problems, such as how to improve efficiency, how to reduce stress and which materials are best suited. Whereas it cost around 7 pence to generate a kilowatt (kW) for one hour using a new oil-fired power station, by 1980 the cost produced by wave power was around 30 pence with Cockerell's raft, and 20 pence with Salter's ducks. Vickers' oscillating water column had produced electricity for as little as 15 pence per kWh and Vickers was exploring two other designs with a possibility of cutting that cost in half. The National Engineering Laboratory at East Kilbride in Scotland had tested its improved wave piston device and attained costs in the 5 to 15 pence range. Lancaster University's flexible bag system appeared to be capable of producing energy at about 8 pence/kWh and possibly as low as 4 pence/kWh according to one independent report in 1979, while Lancaster Polytechnic's clam has produced energy at a cost of only 6 pence/kWh.

The problem is not only how to achieve the government's target of 5 pence/kWh (coal costs only 3.5 pence/kWh), but also to obtain a system that wears well at sea – that is reliable without costing too much in maintenance and repair. But that wave-generated electricity could be a realistic goal must now be beyond reasonable doubt.

Think of what it would mean to solve the problem properly; a renewable energy source which does not pollute and which, unlike oil, coal or uranium, would never run out. The source is matched to demand over a yearly cycle: the waves are most energetic in winter when power is most needed. Environmentally it is attractive in that the devices have a low profile and if placed ten miles offshore would not be visible from the land. Their main disadvantage would be the potential hazard to shipping (not a difficult problem to overcome) and the calming of the seas to their lee with possible changes in the ecology of the shoreline. However, that ecology would be changed in any case, as heavy seas tend to move pieces of coast around from time to time.

Heavy seas or ships may damage parts of the wave-power system. However, all the wave-power devices suggested so far are decentralised. That is, the system consists of many independent units. If some are knocked out, the others carry on. Contrast this technology with the problems created when part of a nuclear reactor goes faulty. In addition to gaining an environmentally acceptable energy source, there would be two further advantages. Insofar as the fuel costs are zero, if the devices are designed properly for wear and tear, this form of electricity could be an enormous generator of revenue for the government. Second, if Britain designed the best devices first, there would be a huge market, first the thousand miles around the British Isles, then as a major export item. What a shot in the arm for the heavy engineering and shipbuilding industries! The technology required to build large numbers of wave-power devices is simply a matter of transferring engineering and other skills which are well developed in the UK. Britain ought to pursue wave power in the early 1980s with the same resolution and speed with which she went after RADAR in the early 1940s. Instead, she has been frittering away her technological lead by providing only marginal and erratic support for wave power while expending huge sums on nuclear energy even after doubts have been cast on the latter's economic viability.

COASTAL FISH-FARMING

The harnessing of wave power could be coupled to coastal fish-farming. That is, the calmed ocean waters could be the site for growing shellfish of various sorts and other forms of fish. Here again, the technology is not yet well developed. Coastal fish-farming is clearly practical in warm tropical waters, but there are problems in the cold waters of the North Atlantic. We need more basic research in areas like limnology, oceanography and marine biology. However, even in its absence, there exist rudiments of the practice now for special cases such as salmon farming on the US Pacific coast. Although the great majority of North American salmon hatcheries are state enterprises, private hatcheries using 'sea-ranching' techniques are becoming more common. Both Oregon and Alaska have passed laws permitting their operation, allowing private operators to raise fish from egg to market stage in net-pen culture in confined marine areas.

The main opposition to ocean salmon ranching comes from commercial fishermen who fear competition, and with good reason. Between 1971 and 1977 the number of salmon reared increased from an approximate estimated 50 thousand to 12 million.

The UK is conducting some experiments. These include the marine culture of rainbow trout in Strangford Lough, Northern Ireland, and investigations carried on at the Fisheries Laboratory in Lowestoft on whiting and flatfish (e.g. dabs). A significantly funded research programme should begin to pay dividends in one to two decades – possibly much sooner if the research is good enough and the findings applied with enough vigour to commercial developments.

The second of the major food technologies, single-cell protein, is on the verge of becoming economic. Traditional cattle feed like hay needs to be supplemented with protein in order to grow healthy animals. Single-cell protein consists of protein made by yeast (or other, single-celled, micro-organisms) from organic substances including those derived from oil, agricultural wastes, sawdust or coal. The economic importance of this technology becomes clear when we realise that about half the grain consumed in the UK is consumed by livestock, not by people.

Single-cell protein should be used to increase the production of milk cows with a view to producing cheese. Britain makes some of the most delicious cheeses in the world, but almost nobody outside Britain knows this. Cheeses should become a major export item.

The well-worn piece of folk wisdom which proclaims that Britain must produce manufactured goods for export in order to pay for food imports has no real basis in fact. By continuing to increase productivity in traditional farming, then coupling it to new food sources such as coastal fish-farming and single-cell protein, the British economy could easily become a net exporter of food.

There are a number of emerging technologies which have less direct relevance for Britain but would be important for other parts of the globe. All of these would, of course, affect the British economy as well, directly or indirectly. Of particular interest are those technologies which utilise the oceans for food, minerals and energy.

The idea of coastal fish-farming described for the British Isles is immediately practical for the warmer tropical shorelines of the world. The limiting factor is not research, but development, including ways and means of introducing it in a practical way. One scheme being investigated by the United Nations involves mussel culture. Mussel larvae, in order to grow and complete their life-cycle, must attach themselves to some object in the water, like rocks or pier pilings. In many parts of the world this is the limiting factor. Mussel farming consists of setting up rafts from which ropes hang down into the water. The larvae attach themselves to these ropes which can be hauled up every few weeks, stripped of mussels and returned to the water for the next 'crop'. Under optimum conditions, one estimate indicates that as much as 150 tons of flesh can be produced per hectare each year. This would produce 25 tons of fishmeal. Contrast this with the 750 kg of beef per hectare from the best pasture land coupled to supplemental feeding. The mussels could be used for human consumption, but their main value would be as protein supplement for chickens, pigs and other livestock. The shells, in turn, could be used for lime for agricultural purposes and as a base for road building and construction materials.

What makes the system so attractive for the Third World is that it is labour intensive and not capital intensive. The rafts and ropes can be made from local materials. The main cost would be in the form of old tyres filled with air to provide the extra buoyancy necessary to counter the weight of the ropes laden with mussels. Local fishing boats, currently in use, could make the harvest runs. The old folks, women and children could be employed to husk the shells and to work in the canning factories, and each family could support some chickens and pigs fed by the mussels.

OCEAN FARMING

The oceans, as a whole, have an enormous potential for producing plants which could be cropped. Most of the solar energy received at the earth's surface is absorbed by the upper layers of the oceans, which cover 70 per cent of the earth. The surface waters which absorb this sunshine tend to be 'biological deserts' because they are very low in nitrates and phosphates needed for plant growth. However, ocean waters below 100–300 metres generally contain these nutrients at relatively high concentrations. If the two could be combined under controlled conditions, by far more food could be grown in the oceans than is presently grown on land.

Such a scheme has been worked out by H. A. Wilcox of the Naval Ocean Systems Center in San Diego. Wilson points to the three main reasons why open oceans are not farmed: first, the natural bottom is too deep; second, the natural surface waters carry insufficient nutriments; and third, the hazard of storms. Wilcox resolves these difficulties by: developing an open-work mesh of stout plastic lines 15 to 30 metres below the surface to which seaweed may attach; providing intake pipes which reach 100 to 300 metres down into the nutrient-rich layers of the ocean and pumping this enriched water up, using the motion of the waves to provide the energy for pumping; and carefully selecting sites and using up-to-date ocean engineering techniques for reducing the risks from storms. The crop plant Wilcox has in mind is the giant California kelp which is already being grown and cropped in the coastal waters of California. The seaweed would be harvested periodically by ships using large clippers to cut the tops of the fronds one or two metres below the surface. The kelp tops will grow again after each harvest so that such a seafarm need be 'planted' only once.

Strands of kelp provide a natural ecosystem for many other creatures. The ocean farms could be made to yield harvests of oysters and fin fish as well. Dried kelp can be digested by sheep with about the same efficiency as normal base rations of alfalfa hay, oat hay, barley and sodium phosphate. Alternatively, it could be used for agar, or as an organic base for chemicals and methane production. The whole experimental project was initiated by the US Navy in 1972. The project was turned over to the General Electric Company in 1977 where the programme continues. Whether, or rather when, such a system will become operational depends on the economics of it. On the one hand the cost of producing food and other products by marine culture must continue to fall as advances in technology provide cheaper materials (e.g. plastic lines) and machinery (e.g. wave-powered pumps). On the other hand, the value of the product must increase either because the price of the product goes up (e.g. increases in the price of hay), or of increases in productivity (e.g. the same farm produces both kelp and quality oysters). It is not possible, as yet, to know when the wealth generated by ocean farms will be sufficient to justify their development. However, when they are developed, it will be another example of converting a non-resource, the biological deserts of the ocean's surface waters, into a wealth-creating resource through technology.

DEEP-SEA MINING

The oceans can also become a major source of valuable minerals. At present, ocean mining is confined to the continental shelves. It includes the recovery of tin-bearing minerals (cassiterite) off the coasts of Russia, Thailand and Indonesia, diamonds of Namibia, ironsand off Japan and the Philippines, sulphur in the Gulf of Mexico, and calcium carbonate off the US, the Bahamas, France, Iceland, Fiji and others. The most important solid minerals mined offshore are sand and gravel, accounting for over 40 per cent of the annual production of the global marine mining industry in 1977 (total $460 million). Marine sand and gravel are produced by Japan, the UK, Denmark, Holland, the US, Sweden and others.

However, a new technology, deep-sea mining, is developing rapidly. In the early 1980s the greatest attention will be focussed on the deep sea 'manganese nodules', which constitute one of the largest mineral deposits on this planet. But at the moment the economics are such that only a small percentage of nodule deposits are a viable mining proposition. These occur mainly between the Clarion and Clipper Fraction Zones in the equatorial North Pacific. A number of countries including the US, Canada, Japan, Germany, France, Belgium, Holland and the UK are carrying out exploratory programs. The limiting factor by 1980 was not so much the technology or the economic potential, but international law. Who owned these sites? The fear expressed by one official of a company concerned with exploration was: 'We develop the operation, then out of the blue there appears a Peruvian gunboat to take over the whole thing . . .'

This statement illustrates an important point: converting non-resources (such as manganese nodules at the bottom of the Pacific) into wealth-generating resources requires not only technological but also organisational, expertise. At this point, the problems of mining the nodules are a mix of technological, political, economic, and legal ones.

When all these are solved, the manganese nodules will provide a new source of wealth for the world. Doubly so, for contained within these nodules is not only manganese, but also iron, copper, nickel, and cobalt. Further technology will take advantage of these 'impurities' in the manganese nodules.

As deep-sea mining technology evolves, coupled with automated mining developments on land, the stage will be set for tapping potential mineral resources in Antarctica and other remote areas of the world (as with North Alaska oil). Ultimately that experience, coupled to space technology, will make it possible to mine the moon, the asteroids and the planets.

Technology has, in the past, created wealth by generating steam power, electricity, the internal combustion engine and other energy devices. Similarly, wealth was created from entirely new materials such as plastics, fibreglass and new ceramics. This process is accelerating. Theoretical knowledge in organic chemistry makes it feasible to design new molecules with properties to specifications. As our knowledge expands the world gets wealthier. It is not until we understand that the major increases in a society's wealth occur when technology transforms a non-resource into a resource – it is not until then that we can devise a successful economy. Whether it is converting woodland to farmland, draining the sea, using titanium for high-temperature steel alloys, or whatever, the new products and services come into being as a result of ideas in people's heads. It is the combination of entrepreneurial ability, technological know-how and workforce skills which are a society's greatest economic asset. 'Knowledge is power.' It also creates wealth.

5 The silicon revolutions and deserts which bloom

'Gold and silver, as they are naturally of the greatest value among the richest, so they are naturally of the least value among the poorest nations. Among savages, the poorest of all nations, they are of scarce any value.'

Adam Smith, Book One, Chapter XI.

What is the most valuable substance in the world today? Gold? Silver? Platinum? Diamonds? No. Quartz probably is. Gold, platinum and diamonds are valuable because they are rare. As such they have been given a high value and are expensive. But what can you do with a small amount of gold? You can buy and sell it and make money by speculating on its rising price. But the money-making (wealth-creating) potential of such a piece of gold is very limited. What can you do with quartz? You can use the silicon in it to make a micro-processor which becomes the centre of a system which can become a great wealth creator. Alternatively the quartz can be turned into photovoltaic cells which generate electricity for as long as the sun shines. It is in fact possible to combine these two functions as is being done with devices ranging from solar-powered pocket calculators to communications satellites. The wealth-creating possibility of quartz is much greater than that of gold.

Consider for a moment the enormous productive potential of an advanced silicon chip of the type appearing in the mid-1980s. The total labour input into producing that single chip is trivial and, considering the price of that chip, so is the capital input. On the other hand, the information input has been enormous and represents a history of accumulated knowledge.

One might argue that to obtain such a powerful device at such low costs and with such little human effort required huge expenditures and efforts in order to develop the chip in the first place. However, that capital outlay and labour expended largely represents an effort to obtain the information necessary for creating and developing the chip. It was that build up of information which allowed a small sliver of silicon weighing less than a gram to become the 'brain' of a powerful computer producing, potentially, tens of thousands of pounds of services and revenues annually. It becomes one of the major intellectual tasks of economists to try to assign monetary value to the role of information in the economy. One place to begin is to define value added in terms of their information inputs.The ability to use a material is a function of knowledge. Wealth from knowledge has many forms – here we will concentrate on that resulting from the silicon revolution.

The first silicon revolution consisted of converting quartz into information devices – the silicon chips. The second revolution involves the conversion of quartz into energy transducing devices – the photovoltaic cells. The third silicon revolution will convert desert sand (which is mostly quartz) into a glass-house – the core of a new technological system which, just as the deep plough transformed northern Europe a thousand years ago, will make the deserts bloom.

THE FIRST SILICON REVOLUTION: CHIPS

As with all evolutionary processes, it is difficult to pinpoint the precise beginning of the silicon revolution. Knowledge builds on previous knowledge. Nothing in human history begins without antecedents. But sometimes there are discontinuities in the process of information building. The studies of Michael Faraday in the 1830s surely represent one such discontinuity. In 1831 Faraday demonstrated that moving a piece of wire through a magnetic field would generate an electric current. This discovery of 'electromagnetic induction' was rapidly taken up by other investigators and before the century was out gave rise not only to many academic studies, but created several new meta-technologies such as electric motors, electric lights, the telephone and the major industries associated with these developments. These advances also provided the foundation for the electronics industry. In 1833 Faraday made another, rather puzzling, discovery. Whereas the ease with which electricity could pass through a material such as copper and silver decreased with heating, the ability of silver sulphide, rather a poor conductor to start with, to pass on electric current, actually increased with heating. Pure copper, silver and a number of other metals are good 'conductors' of electricity. Silver sulphide was the first 'semi-conductor' to be investigated. It took about a century before enough information and understanding had been accumulated both to define the term 'semi-conductor' precisely and to understand what was going on. It was the theoretical understanding of solid-state physics in the 1930s which set the stage for the development of transistors in the late 1940s.

The transistors are semi-conductor devices which displaced the earlier electronic vacuum tubes, frequently called valves because, like valves, they regulated the flow of electrons. The transistor, then, is a crystal of semi-conductive material in which small flows of electrons can be controlled to provide signals. A number of materials, and combinations of materials, have been shown to work, but most of the technology of the last couple of decades has centred on crystals of very pure silicon which have been 'doped' with small amounts of some other element such as boron or phosphorus to give the crystal just the right electronic properties. As the German physicist R.W. Pohl had predicted in the 1930s, small crystals (the transistors) began replacing the electronic valves during the 1950s.

Among the first large-scale applications of the transistor was the transistor radio. This, however, was still made the way radios were always made. You started with a metal chassis and you placed on this chassis (properly insulated) the various electronic components: resistors, capacitors, transformers, etc., including the transistors. You then wired the whole lot together. This was a slow, laborious process. Like calculating lengthy sums with pencil and paper – there ought to be a better way.

Enter the integrated circuit. As Professor Ernest Braun, Head of Aston University's Technology and Policy Unit, has pointed out, the integrated circuit was a commercial innovation developed largely by and within industry (in contrast to the transistor which, except for the very last steps, was developed in university and basic research laboratories). Instead of soldering wires to various components on a metal chassis in order to connect them, you began with a board made of plastic (or other non-conducting material) onto which you sprayed a pattern of thin strips of metallic conducting material. This created a printed circuit board into which you could insert the components. Around 1960 this principle began to be extended to spraying conducting materials onto parts of silicon wafers themselves. The silicon chip revolution was beginning.

What is a chip? How is it made? A chip is the equivalent of a printed circuit board ingeniously created on a small sliver of silicon (i.e. on a silicon chip). Remember that the printed circuit board for a computer involves mainly electronic 'on/off' switches and is therefore less complicated than a radio. During the 1960s the guts (brains?) of a computer, the processor of information, consisting of batteries of such switches, became miniaturised to the point where each switch consisted of a mere microscopic spot on the silicon chip. The information processor had become a micro-processor. The 'mighty micro' had arrived.

How is a micro-processor made? The process begins with growing very pure, large crystals of silicon. Cylinders of such pure silicon are then sawed like a log into thin wafers, as thin as a knife blade and about the size of the palm of an adult hand. These are then treated in a series of steps which first give the surface and the interior the proper electronic qualities, then photoetch different patterns onto the wafers. The patterns actually involve several hundred identical copies across the wafer such that each wafer produces hundreds of small, square units. Each unit, only a couple of millimetres on edge, contains tens of thousands of microscopic (and even sub-microscopic) switches and other electronic elements. This is the micro-processor. The latest techniques involve beams of atoms, electrons and X-rays which will allow a million electronic elements to be placed on a single chip ... a miracle of production, and a miracle of information power.

THE SECOND SILICON REVOLUTION: PHOTOVOLTAICS

So much for the first silicon revolution. The second involves photovoltaic cells, devices which convert light into electricity. It began in 1839 with Becquerel's observation that light shining on certain combinations of metals and salts (i.e. potential semi-conductors) produced electricity. The formal theoretical understanding for this phenomenon was provided in 1905 by Albert Einstein (who, incidentally, won the Nobel prize for his work on the photoelectric effect and not for the theory of relativity). By the 1930s work carried out in Pohl's laboratory established the concept that electrons in crystals of poor conductors were normally tightly bound to their parent atoms. These electrons, however, could be loosened by light energy absorbed by the crystal. If an electric field was applied, or some other appropriate means were provided, these freed electrons could then start to move as an electric current.

As the semi-conductor technology developed, so did the photovoltaic technology. In 1954 the Bell Telephone Laboratories, originator of the transistor, devised the modern photovoltaic solar cell. The new cells were made from single crystals of silicon, doped to give them the right electronic properties. They achieved a solar energy conversion efficiency of about 10 per cent, but their theoretical maximum would be closer to 25 per cent. The first international conference on solar energy was held in 1956. The new solar cells generated considerable excitement but the economics were terrible. It would cost $200 to generate one watt of electricity in full sunlight.

The launching of Sputnik in 1957 saved the solar cells from temporary extinction. The US entered the space race. Costs were no more important than in the arms race. Solar photovoltaic cells were ideal for providing the small amounts of power needed for the early satellites. The learning curve was beginning. NASA and the Department of Defense began spending about $2 million a year on photovoltaic power supplies. By 1968

about $25 million had been spent – peanuts compared to the
$500 million spent by that time on trying to create a nuclear
power pack for space vehicles. An advisory committee (on which
nuclear power specialists outnumbered the solar power specialists by about eight to one) recommended that NASA abandon
the space nuclear programme and shift to photovoltaics. NASA
did. By 1974 Skylab took to orbit, and once there, generated
25,000 watts by means of solar cells. A vindication of Joseph
Loferski and other solar enthusiasts who had worked so hard on
NASA.

In the meantime the Arab countries threatened to cut oil
supplies and in any case, the world was beginning to run out of
cheap oil. Solar energy was beginning to look more attractive
to the enlightened, although the vast majority of power engineers still had their heads in the sand. No power projections to
the year 2000 took solar energy seriously. However, a programme for developing terrestrial photovoltaic power systems
had already been launched in 1972, although with a trivial $2
million per year support. That support increased substantially
as oil became more expensive. The 1978 solar photovoltaic act
encouraged the US Department of Energy to undertake a ten-
year $1.5 billion programme to develop various solar cell sys-
tems.

According to one estimate, the world's total terrestrial production of electricity from photovoltaic cells amounted to 50
kilowatts in 1975. Enough to supply a few households. By 1978
it had risen to 2000. Louis Rosenblum and co-workers from the
Lewis Research Centre of the US National Aeronautics and
Space Administration have observed that the cost of solar cells
dropped from $US 35 per peak watt to $13 in three years. They
estimated that the costs of the installed module generating tens
of kilowatts would drop further from the $13 in 1978 to a mere
61 cents in 1986, and that the energy costs per kilowatt-hour
would drop from $2.33 to 47 cents. At that point solar cells
would clearly be the least expensive source for all decentralised
forms of electrical generation.

Such a forecast is not way out of line with earlier forecasts made in the mid-1970s. Assuming that such forecasts are over-enthusiastic, will the price per kilowatt-hour drop to below 50 cents in 1987? 1988? 1989? Furthermore, the forecasts assume a drop in the price as a result of larger production runs – from 'economics of scale' and from the learning curve. The forecasts do not consider further major advances in technology. Yet there are several possibilities which include the way the crystals of silicon are produced. At the moment they are grown in cylindrical shapes, then sawn into thin wafers. A third is lost in sawdust. If it became possible to grow the crystals as a sheet in the first place, it would allow cheaper production and better configurations. This possibility is being explored by Westinghouse. By 1984 Westinghouse plan to build a new semi-automated production line for delivering panels totalling one megawatt of electricity that year.

Many other companies are entering the field, Chevron, Boeing Aerospace, Radio Corporation of America (RCA) and Standard Oil of Ohio (SOHIO) in the US, Sanyo Electric and Fuji Electric in Japan, AEG-Telefunken in Germany, ENI, Italy's huge state-owned oil company, to mention only a few. SOHIO has signed a joint-venture agreement with Energy Conversion Devices which claims that they will be able to produce cells for 33 cents per peak watt.

Another approach involves the use of cheap plastic lenses to focus more sunlight onto the photovoltaics. Covering material developed at the Hebrew University in Jerusalem converts the sunlight into wavelengths more suitable to the photocell, thereby increasing the efficiency still further. A third approach, and one of the most promising, involves the transfer of information from the first to the second silicon revolution. That is, the technology developed for producing the chip could be applied to producing more sophisticated and efficient photovoltaic devices. There is a whole new class of solar cells called conductor-insulator-semiconductor (CIS). A decade is a long time in this field. It would be surprising if there were no further developments in the 1980s so that by the 1990s the price of electricity from solar photovoltaics would have dropped enough for it to become cheaper than either fossil fuel or nuclear energy for those countries with an ample supply of sunshine.

The impact of this technology will be dramatic. The first impact is likely to be in the US and other affluent countries which have plenty of sunshine. The largest single consumer of electricity in the US is air-conditioning. Solar energy is perfectly matched to that demand – a lot of sunshine and a great need for air-conditioning go hand in hand. Other uses will follow. These will range from general power generation to transport. Already we have seen the flight of a photovoltaic-powered aeroplane, the *Solar Challenger*, across the English Channel on a clear July day. Its inventor, Paul MacCready, was quoted as saying, 'It's actually the most ridiculous use I can think of for solar cells . . . We just wanted to point out dramatically how much solar power can do.' That may be true for 1981. But what happens when photovoltaics get very cheap? Can an aeroplane designer of a trans-Atlantic jetliner afford not to coat the upper surfaces of the plane with the photovoltaics to provide the power once the plane has climbed above the clouds?

Most important, however, will be the impact on the Third World countries. One thing most of them have a lot of is sunshine. It has been the Third World economies which have been hit the hardest by rises in oil price. For example, in 1974 the rise in oil price wiped out India's hard-won trade surpluses. To understand what cheap photovoltaics will mean to poorer parts of the world let us examine the world's first village to be powered by solar cells, on the western edge of the Papago Indian Reservation in Arizona. The village, consisting of ninety-five people in fifteen families, was about seventeen miles from the nearest electric facility. The villagers' traditional diet consisted of beans, tortillas, chillies and commercial non-perishable vegetable and tinned foods. Wild game and cattle provided an occasional supplement. The food pattern reflected, in part, the absence of refrigeration. Water was provided by a diesel-powered pump, while lighting was by kerosene lamps and candles.

The experiment began on 16 December 1978. The photovoltaics provided electricity not only for pumping water and supplying lights in the homes and community buildings, but also for family refrigerators, a communal washing machine and a sewing machine. Life became easier, nutrition better.

Similarly the village of Tangaye, 120 miles east of Ouagadougou, the capital of Upper Volta, found life a lot easier after a solar photovoltaic-powered grain mill and water pump were installed. The mill was particularly welcomed by the women who used to have to pound the grain (sorghum and millet) with a large wooden mortar and pestle into coarse flour, and to stone grind by hand to obtain the fine flour. This arduous task generally took about two hours per day.

In October 1981 the world's largest photovoltaic power plant came on line to provide electricity for two isolated Saudi Arabian villages. As part of the $100-million 'Soleras' agreement, signed in 1977 between the Saudi Arabian National Centre for Science and Technology and the US Departments of Energy and Treasury, supplying the power plant was part of a programme designed to explore several aspects of solar energy. Although producing only a very modest 350 kW at that time (planned to be upgraded to 1,000 kW), the plant provided a great deal of practical engineering experience under desert conditions. Most important, all the Soleras projects involve university students with a view to training a core of Saudi engineers and technicians so that the second generation of solar devices will evolve out of a national solar science programme.

The main impact of solar-powered photovoltaics will not be on family comforts but on agriculture and small industry. Most farms in developing countries have water available at less than ten metres below the ground. The pumps, therefore, need only 1000 watts or less. Such pumps are being developed and tested under the auspices of the UN Development Programme. Pumps powered by the heat of the sun are also being developed, particularly in India. Cheap reliable electricity for irrigation pumps and farm machinery as well as for food processing industries will greatly increase the productivity of the poorer parts of the world. The second silicon revolution, the development of cheap photovoltaics, will become a classic example of technology creating wealth by developing a non-resource, sunshine, into a major resource, useful energy.

MAKING THE DESERTS BLOOM

About a fifth of the world's land area is classed as desert. In addition to outright desert, there are vast territories of semi-arid land characterised by marginal productivity and periodic droughts followed by famine. About one out of eight people on this planet live on desert or semi-arid lands – lands which are the source of so much human misery.

The proper application of technical and managerial know-how could transform deserts, making them major exporters of energy, food and chemicals. The outstanding example is Israel, which has been so successful that, for a time, it was possible to distinguish its national boundaries from the air: green on one side, brown on the other. Other states in the Middle East have at least as much land, have or could obtain the necessary labour, have no shortage of capital and would have no trouble finding the necessary materials and energy. Yet these areas have remained barren. Contrast the educational and technological levels of the Israelis with those of the other states. The most important input in this case is information.

The transformation of deserts from low to high productivity calls for: utilising three-dimensional agriculture at the perimeter of the desert areas where there is some water; the use of solar energy for pumping sub-surface water or water from other sources, including sea water, into the drier areas, and the use of crop plants particularly adapted to such conditions; and using the hard-core desert areas for a high-technology transformation, at the heart of which is the use of solar energy, first to produce cheap glass-houses from desert materials, and second to pump in sea water which is then converted to fresh water and valuable chemicals. Let us look at these proposals in more detail.

THREE-DIMENSIONAL AGRICULTURE

The idea of 'three-dimensional agriculture' involves the use of food-yielding trees for crops and the use of their products for feeding livestock. The trees are valuable in themselves as a source of firewood or timber, their leaves are edible to cattle, while their fruit may be used for human consumption, or as protein-rich fodder.

Among the most promising species are the tree legumes, in particular, the carob (*Caratonia siliqua*) and the algaroba (*Prosopis* sp.). The carob is native to the eastern Mediterranean and is especially important to the economy of Cyprus where the seeds are used for the making of adhesives for export. The tree is drought-resistant, starts to bear from four to eight years and may remain productive for over a hundred years. It is evergreen and bears pods which are not only valuable fattening and nourishing food for cattle, but can also be ground into flour for human consumption. The seeds may be used as a substitute for coffee, while the sweet mucilaginous pulp is sold as a confection called 'St John's Bread'. A stand of good-quality carob trees can yield as much as 20 tons of fodder per acre annually. The main disadvantage is that these trees need care in the early stages of planting the forests.

The algaroba originated in the New World and comprises many species. Most favour warm climates but some can withstand frosts. Hawaii has over 50,000 acres of these trees under cultivation, with a total yield of as much as 1 million tons of fodder per year. The algaroba is quick-growing and the pods may be ground into a highly nutritious meal, good for cattle and human consumption alike. The tree is of medium size and tolerates dry waste places. The wood is a satisfactory fuel and the lumber is used for piles. The bark contains tannin as well as a gum suitable for varnish and glue and as a medicine for dysentery. The pale yellow flowers are a source of delicious honey and apiculture, using newer breeds of stingless bees, should be an automatic adjunct to the leguminous forest farm.

A wide variety of livestock may be reared on a forest farm. Not only the more usual cattle, sheep, pigs and goats, but certain game animals such as elands and rabbits may also be cultivated profitably. Poultry, like rabbits, have the advantage of being allowed free range throughout the woodlands. By moving standard portable electric fences, one could rotate the larger livestock around the forest farm to prevent overgrazing which strips the land of its ground cover.

Exposed land creates a much harsher environment for all forms of life: deprived of shade, it heats up much more during the day, while at night, deprived of its infra-red retaining cover, the earth tends to freeze. The increase in ground-level wind velocities causes the top layers of soil to dry rapidly. Furthermore, increasing daytime temperatures cause an increase in microbial activity leading to an increased rate of decomposition of organic matter. Organic nitrogen is converted to soluble ammonia or nitrates which the occasional rains quickly leach away. The loss of fertility sets the stage for irreversible changes. The land becomes extremely vulnerable to cyclic climatological shifts involving periods of decreased rainfall. Unless a plant cover is regenerated fast enough after grazing, the land is exposed to erosion by wind and water. The combined impact of decreased rainfall, erosion, decreased moisture-retaining capacity, decreased fertility and increased diurnal temperature variations leads to a new ecological equilibrium – the desert.

Establishing a forest of tree legumes can reverse the process. The microclimate at the soil surface is immediately ameliorated by the tree cover – temperatures are cooler during the day and warmer at night, while the surface soil moisture is substantially increased. Because these tree legumes have the ability to fix nitrogen, organic nitrogen is actually increased in the soil when the trees are harvested for timber. Arid soils in regions of bright sunlight are frequently rich in minerals but suffer from nitrogen deficiency. Once soil fertility, temperature and moisture have been sufficiently restored, drought-resistant grasses can be grown. Where needed, artificial nitrogen supplements obtained by means of solar energy (as described later) may be applied. The nitrogen balance would be further improved by working into the soil the manure of grazing livestock.

Three-dimensional agriculture need not be confined to a few species of trees and grasses, but can embrace all kinds of combi-

nations of plants and animals likely to produce drought-resistant ecosystems of high productivity.

In this connection the jojoba nut has immense commercial
potential. The jojoba bush grows wild in the south-western US
and Mexico, and is cultivated experimentally there and in parts
of the Middle East. The oil expressed from this nut is a light
'liquid wax' which can be used in delicate machinery such as
watches. At the moment the major source of such oil is the
sperm whale, and the jojoba oil can substitute for it in paper
coatings, polishes, electrical insulation, carbon paper, textiles,
leather, precision casting, pharmaceuticals and other purposes.
Extensive plantings of the jojoba nut might therefore save this
whale from extinction.

In addition, jojoba plantations might set the pattern for
supplying the industrial world with a source of oil which is
renewable. The natural life span of a jojoba plant appears to be
more than 100 years, perhaps 200. The plant grows best in
well-drained coarse desert soils with 15–18 inches of rainfall,
but it also develops well in areas with an annual rainfall of 8
inches, and it even occurs in areas where rainfall is less than 5
inches. The seeds produce not only the oil but, following extraction, a pulp consisting of 25 per cent high-quality edible
protein. Plantations in the US and Israel indicate that the yield
would be one to 2,000 lb of oil per acre.

A second plant which could yield oil in commercial quantities
is *Copaifera langsdorffii*. This tree yields oil the way a rubber tree
yields latex. Like the carob and algaroba trees, *Copaifera* is a
legume capable of fixing atmospheric nitrogen. Stands of such
trees, therefore, enrich the soil as they grow. Breeding experiments to further improve yields of oil or other desirable qualities,
such as drought resistance, have only just begun. The potential
for 'growing' oil is real, however.

Practical experience in reclaiming wasteland by means of
three-dimensional agriculture, or checking the spread of deserts, is rapidly accumulating. Algarobas are being planted in
India under United Nations auspices along a belt 400 miles long
and two miles wide (that is, about half a million acres) to check

the spread of the Thar and Rajputana deserts. Similar trials are being conducted at several sites in central and eastern Africa. In the Sudan there are not only major engineering projects to smooth out the annual water flows of the Upper Nile, but extensive tree plantings have taken place as well. At Berber the trees in new shelter belts did so well that their seeds have naturally regenerated the shelter belt on the desert side under very arid conditions. The tree which appears to be most promising under these conditions is the mesquite (*Prosopis juliflora*) which can tolerate quite high levels of salinity in soil and survive heavy browsing by goats and sheep. It too produces pods which are suitable protein supplements for animals. The goats spread the seeds, thereby extending the shelter belt. Acacia, eucalyptus and carob trees are also being planted in the shelter belts. The eucalyptus are planted on the sheltered side to be cropped for timber. The Sudanese government hopes to transform the country into the breadbasket of the Arab world. Many governments are in the process of reclaiming arid lands. Unfortunately, most of the schemes rely on large quantities of fresh water involving major irrigation schemes. These require large investment of capital and materials such as concrete, steel and complex machinery, which, in turn, often depend on expensive fuel.

WATER SHORTAGES

Several approaches are feasible. All are dependent on massive inputs of energy, presumably solar energy, although under certain circumstances other energy sources might also be considered (e.g. geothermal energy or wind power). The first involves the use of solar energy pumps to pump up water from deep underground sources which are known to exist. The second involves pumping salt water from the sea and desalinating it in large quantities. This second alternative might be used to supplement the intermediate technology of the first. For example, should local irrigation endanger the level of the water table, then supplementing the system with imported water might be desirable.

Actually one can mix fresh and salt water as an increasing number of crop plants have been bred for salt tolerance. Professor S. M. Siegel and colleagues of the Department of Botany, University of Hawaii, have demonstrated that certain varieties of maize plants, grown on half-diluted sea water, flowered and produced normal seed in both fresh and brackish water. Chinese cabbage, tomato and bell pepper cultivars can be grown in good yield when irrigated with up to 40 per cent sea water. The Hawaii group believe that both barley and rye could be bred for sea water agriculture.

There are at least two types of technology capable of utilising solar energy for providing the large amounts of power needed for water pumps. The first uses collectors such as a 5–6 ft parabolic mirror which focuses the sun's rays on the boilers of a Stirling hot air engine. As Farrington Daniels has pointed out, various types of Stirling engines and focussing collectors could probably be mass produced at low cost once the demand became sufficiently large. Such pumps would only handle small quantities of water, but in view of their low operating cost might be scattered throughout the farm, possibly even to supply individual trees via underground polyethylene tubing (drip irrigation). They would also serve as drinking fountains for people and animals. The pumps would not work well during cloudy weather, but would not be needed as much since cloudy weather often means rain anyway.

The second type of pump would be conventionally powered by electricity, the electricity being provided by photovoltaic cells. This technology may prove to be more practical initially, although in the long run direct solar pumps might turn out to be more efficient and economical.

A major feasibility study of both types of pump was begun in July 1979 under the auspices of the World Bank acting for the UN Development Programme. The consortium of knowledge producers consists of Sir William Halcrow and Parkrees in association with the Intermediate Technology Group of London, the Solar Energy Unit of University College, Cardiff, and other institutions. The field trials are being conducted in co-

operation with research institutions and technical organisations
of India, Mali, the Philippines and Sudan.

At present only about 8 per cent of the earth's land surface is
suitable for the profitable growing of field crops by conventional methods. The use of three-dimensional agriculture,
coupled to solar energy-based irrigation systems, could convert
semi-arid wastelands into highly productive lands, thereby
doubling global food supplies. In the long run, however, we
will have to move deeper into the hard-core deserts.

THE THIRD SILICON REVOLUTION: DESERT GLASS-HOUSES

The heart of the proposed desert production system is the
glass-house designed as a solar still. The glass-house is to be
partially sunk into the ground so that only the glass A-frame or
the fibreglass inverted-U frame projects above the soil line. The
floor of the glass-house is dug into the desert soil itself and so are
the 'benches'. That is, the house would be open to the ground
and so taking advantage of what soil moisture there exists. The
glass top is sealed shut most of the time so as to trap all moisture
and the inner glass surfaces are used to collect the condensing
moisture as water droplets. Rows of growing plants alternate
with troughs made of blackened solar-absorptive materials filled
with sea water or some other source of brackish or salt water.
The sun causes the water to evaporate, the moisture is collected
on the glass surfaces and would run off into collecting troughs
at the inner sides of the house, from whence it is distributed to
the plants by gravity feed, drip irrigation using underground
polyethylene fibreglass tubes or the most recent, and potentially
most productive technique for certain crops (e.g. tomatoes),
nutrient film irrigation. This technique requires the least
amount of water, yet produces the greatest yield. Developed by
A. J. Cooper of the Glasshouse Crops Research Institute in
Littlehampton (UK), the technique is based on the use of long,
narrow sheets of black polythene which are converted into
'gulleys' inside which the plant roots grow in a shallow stream
of continually circulating and replenished nutrient solution.
The roots grow in a moisture-saturated atmosphere which pro-

vides them with water and oxygen simultaneously, plus a perfectly designed mix of minerals to support plant growth. Pest problems in isolated, sealed glass-houses surrounded by deserts would be minimal.

The use of glass-houses in desert regions is increasing by leaps and bounds: Arab, Israeli and Soviet projects are not only designed to produce food, but also to provide desalination. If capital can be found to build a vast network of desert glass-houses there is no reason why the deserts of the world should not become a major supplier of high-quality fresh fruits and vegetables. However, these technology systems would become economically much more efficient (that is, they would provide a much greater return on capital) if they were coupled to high-level technology systems; for such technology would provide cheap glass, fertiliser and water, and solve the waste salt water problems.

There are many different ways and means of using solar energy. One form which we haven't discussed is solar furnaces. Here the sun's rays are focussed onto a small area to provide intense heat the way one may light a fire with a magnifying glass by focussing the sun onto paper or twigs. A very large device, using parabolic mirrors, has been in operation in the French Pyrenees for many years. It achieves extremely high temperatures. Devices of this sort may be developed for producing glass, quartz, ceramics or whole families of new chemicals whose synthesis requires very high temperature.

Whether by means of solar furnaces, or whether by more traditional means, the key to desert development will be cheap glass. The raw material, sand and salts, are in plentiful supply in desert regions. So are the large amounts of energy required to convert the raw material into glass. The limiting factor is the information required to put the system together properly into economically viable enterprises.

When these and other systems are organised, the deserts will also become a major producer of chemicals including fertilisers. For example, desert glass-houses could be used to extract minerals from sea water. The dissolved salts of sea water contain many minerals. These include potash, aluminium, magnesium and many others, even gold and uranium. At present sea water is not used as a raw material for extracting these chemicals (there are some exceptions such as bromine) because of the high cost of energy required to evaporate the sea water in the first place. In the case of the desert glass-houses, the sea water would be pumped primarily to generate fresh water. The concentrated brine would accumulate as a by-product. It would, of course, become a valuable raw material for a budding inorganic chemicals industry. The presence of cheap electrical energy would permit electric furnaces, electrolysis, electrodyalisis and ion exchange systems to operate economically on the concentrated sea water produced by the glass-houses.

One of the minerals which could be produced from sea water is potash. Many deserts have deposits of phosphates. Last, cheap energy allows the conversion of atmospheric nitrogen into ammonia or nitrates. These three, coupled to the reclamation of trace elements from the sea water, should make possible the production of both standard fertilisers for export and the precise chemical formulations required for nutrient film irrigation.

The most common mineral of the sea, table-salt, could be converted for use with desert sand to make the glass for the greenhouses. Excess fresh water produced could be coupled with excess energy produced by the sun during the day to generate hydrogen and oxygen for export or local storage. It will be the adroit development of these 'interlocking elements' which, like Europe's Agricultural Revolution or the Industrial Revolution, foster entirely new wealth-creating production systems. And it all depends upon knowledge which turns non-resources into resources.

Lest the reader be overwhelmed by the technology and its potential, it may be well to restate the central theme of this book. Wealth is created when a non-resource is converted into a resource as a result of applying information (new or old). In this chapter we considered several such examples. These included converting sunshine into electricity by means of photovoltaic devices, transforming unproductive, arid land into land which yields by means of three-dimensional agriculture and the use of cheap irrigation pumps driven by solar energy; melting desert sands into glass for glass-houses designed to act as solar stills, thereby making the deserts bloom; and condensing sea water in these solar stills to yield valuable minerals. The limiting factor is information. The post-industrial economy will produce the wealth of information to make it all happen.

6 Government: consumer or investor?

'But though the profusion of government must, undoubtedly, have retarded the natural progress of England towards wealth and improvement, it has not been able to stop it.'
                                    Adam Smith, Book Two, Chapter III.

Adam Smith did not like governments. His reasons were straightforward:

> Great nations are never impoverished by private, though they sometimes are by public, prodigality and misconduct ... almost the whole public revenue, is in most countries employed in maintaining unproductive hands ... a numerous and splendid court, a great ecclesiastical establishment, great fleets and armies, who in time of war acquire nothing which can compensate the expense of maintaining them, even while the war lasts. Such people, as they themselves produce nothing, are all maintained by the produce of other men's labour ... Those unproductive hands ... may consume so great a share of their revenue ... that all the frugality and good conduct of individuals may not be able to compensate the waste ... (Book Two, Chapter III).

At first sight, one would have expected Adam Smith to be appalled at the economic involvement of governments in post-industrial economies. How shocking to discover that on average more than a third of personal income ends up in government coffers. Or that for western Europe, the value of taxes and revenues collected is close to 40 per cent of the gross national product.

Governments have become paramount in post-industrial economies, not only in terms of national cash flows, but also in terms of labour utilisation: governments are by far the largest single employer. In Britain between the mid-1960s and

TABLE 6.1

European Community 1976
Gross domestic product (at market prices) and
taxes and actual social contributions

	GDP	Taxes, etc.	Percentage
Eur 9	1,242.5*	479.5	38.6
FR Germany	398.8	153.6	38.5
France	310.1	121.7	39.2
Italy	154.7	51.3	33.2
Netherlands	80.1	37.0	46.2
Belgium	59.1	25.4	43.0
Luxembourg	2.0	1.0	50.0
UK	196.2	72.0	36.7
Ireland	7.1	2.7	38.0
Denmark	34.4	14.9	43.3

*European units of account

mid-1970s the increase in local and national government employment rose from one in seven to one in five – and that does not include nationalised industries and the armed forces. In some parts of the UK, viz. Northern Ireland, by the late 1970s more than one in three people employed were working for the government. The shifting employment patterns of an industrial city like Bradford, between 1975 and 1980 illustrate the point. While the ten largest manufacturing employers lost 5,000 jobs, the ten largest service employers took on 1,500 additional workers. What is so significant is that eight out of these ten are public service employers. The Bradford City Corporation is by far the largest single employer in the region. Second is the Area Health Authority. Others include the Post Office and Telecommunications, the Gas Board, the Yorkshire Electricity Board, West Yorkshire Transport, Bradford University and Bradford College.

It is the purpose of this chapter to examine the economic role of government in a post-industrial economy: is government a waste of money, a legitimate consumer, a service provider, social technology, an investor, or a combination of some of these? The answer provides a key to the way our society can exploit our wealth of information. Adam Smith viewed governments, by

and large, as a waste of money. This is not surprising in view of
the top-heavy and rather unproductive aristocracy associated
with the European governments of his time. It had become
apparent to most intellectuals of the late eighteenth century
that incompetent, sometimes despotic, monarchies were incom-
patible with the emerging industrial society. Improvements in
transport and communication, such as turnpikes, canals and
newspapers, lessened the need for a tightly centralised political
organisation and favoured democratisation. At the same time
the entrepreneurs developing the new machinery and industries
needed to reinvest their profits, not have them drained off to
support an indolent aristocracy. In North America the Thirteen
States united to get rid of the commercial fetters imposed by
the British monarchy. In France the royalty lost touch,
not only with the people, but also with the financial realities.
The monarchy became bankrupt and literally went out of
business.

There is a large body of opinion today which still maintains
the traditional view that most, if not all, government is a waste
of money. This view is encouraged every time one has a tax
official looking over one's shoulder, or has to bother with renew-
ing a vehicle licence, or for some other reason is shelling out
money to the government. It is particularly irksome in business
to be confronted with a mountain of government laws and
regulations. In the business world the image of government
consists of an army of clerks, sending each other memoranda,
conspiring to keep business from carrying out its productive
tasks. One never thinks of 'the government' when one uses a
road, sees a local bobby on the beat, or confers with a teacher
about a child's progress. Government is a stale, indecisive,
meddlesome bureaucracy which is wholly unproductive.

One reason for this impression is that a basic property of any
large organisation is that it sets up bureaucracies as an institutional device for diffusing responsibility and blame. This
happens to be as true for large corporations, foundations and
universities as for government bureaucracies. To a decisive, self-
made entrepreneur, or to any person who is creative and used

to working in small groups – dealing with government bureaux can be maddening.

The institutional diffusion of responsibility in large organisations makes them slow to respond to changing circumstances and new needs. However, if there does exist a certain amount of outdated and needless paperwork in western governmental bureaucracies, one need only go to Third World countries, inexperienced in maintaining effective bureaucracies, to see what a real shambles can be made of modern productive systems in the absence of effective governmental coordination. One example is that of a shipload of cement left uncovered on the docks because no provision had been made either to move it to its destination or have it properly stored. The rains came . . .

Anyone with extensive Third World experience knows of the lack of managerial training in many government departments and the enormous misappropriation and sheer waste of valuable resources. Yet even in the agrarian and industrial economies of Third World countries, the government is not merely a waste of money. It is vital to the economic well-being of each country. The question is not whether governments are needed, but how to make them more efficient.

GOVERNMENT AS SERVICE PROVIDER

The reason why governments absorb an ever-increasing share of the GNP is that they can do certain things better. Take a few categories of activities which the British government (local or national) engages in such as sewage disposal, the building and maintenance of roads, education, health care, or coal production. Any of these services can be, and have been, provided for by private companies. There are disadvantages, however: building an effective sewage disposal system can be very costly. When the population density is low, each house can have its own pit or cess pool. As the density builds up, this becomes less practical. If the matter were left in private hands, the wealthy areas could afford to install an effective system – the poor could not. This would, sooner or later, lead to outbreaks of cholera, typhoid and other infectious diseases in the poorer areas. The impact on the wealthier sector of the community would be threefold. First, there would exist the distinct possibility of the epidemic spilling over – that is, there would be a direct public health threat. Second, such epidemics lead to social and economic disruption: the labour force becomes unreliable, streets become unsafe, etc. Third, there is, in addition to the threat to the physical well-being of the wealthy, the psychological problems created by observing suffering in one's own community. For although it is true that human beings have no end of stratagems for inuring themselves to other people's suffering, it becomes more and more difficult, the closer to home it happens – at least if there seem to be practical ways of solving the problem; better to install an effective city-wide sewer system. Thus the private system is displaced by a public one.

The building of turnpikes and toll roads by private entre-preneurs has an ancient and venerable history. The same is true for canals and railways. But standards varied enor-mously. As a national economy developed during the industrial era, a national transportation network became increasingly necessary. Not only was it necessary to develop uniform stan-dards, but also to make certain that less favoured, poorer, or more distant parts were tied into the network. Last, in all of these considerations there is the economy-of-scale factor. The greater the number of units provided, the cheaper the cost per unit.

This economy of scale probably provides the reason for many other government activities as well. Large scale means cheaper costs per unit. The result is a system which must be standardised and coordinated and which must reach the disadvantaged parts of the local or national community. This last is true for the provision of education and health care. Historically, we have had the experience that wholly private education or health-care systems do not reach the poorer members of society. For altruis-tic reasons alone, therefore, society would have developed public education and health-care systems. However, there was also the added economic incentive that an educated and healthy workforce is a more productive one.

The same considerations apply to government providing services like police and fire protection, building roads, harbours and airports, and developing the statistical basis for decision-making by collecting reams of data. To consider the government's extensive involvement in a nation's economy as a waste of money obviously overlooks the many services provided by the government. All that may be argued is that many of these services could be run more efficiently by private enterprise. One can point to the United States where both telephone and electricity are provided by private companies. However, both of these private enterprises are carefully regulated by public commissions.

There is no clear evidence that public service corporations run as part of the government are any more or less efficient than large monopolistic private enterprises regulated by public agencies. The key factor usually turns out to be the quality of the management. The main problem is that power corrupts and the whole monolithic system (whether a government-backed monopoly or a state monopoly) tends to become inefficient and self-serving. One of the best ways to break up such power is to allow competition. Another is to have an educated clientele which knows how to complain and get things changed.

The nationalising of industries such as coal or steel, on the other hand, reflects other considerations. Here there is the need to preserve jobs and to stabilise the industry as a whole. Small companies, or individual pits or plants, not able to weather a recession individually, can do so collectively, particularly with government financial support. With the ownership of national enterprises, the government can begin to counteract inflation or recession by contracting or expanding investment and production. In this case, the government begins to be used not merely as a provider of services, but as an instrument of economic policy.

GOVERNMENT AS SOCIAL TECHNOLOGY

Initially the institution of government evolved to solve problems of law and order, and defence. Government was an institution to coordinate larger societies, particularly with a view to reducing internal violence, and for providing protection from outside predation. It is not surprising, therefore, that the head of early governments, be it chief, king, or emperor, usually acted as both the chief justice, and the supreme military commander. As society evolved, a single head ruled over an increasing number of people, and larger and larger territories. To reinforce the stability of the system, organised religion evolved to support the authority of the ruler. Rulers became deities, were made out to be descendants of the Sun God or of similar divine origin, and as such became not only the warrior chief, and chief justice, but the religious head as well. As society evolved, so did the institution of government.

There still exists today a significant body of opinion which believes that the functions of government should be confined to law and order and to defence. To them, the very idea of using the government to regulate the economy is anathema. They cling to a tradition which says that the best government is the one which governs least. This *laissez-faire* approach was part of the legacy of Adam Smith and made sense in the early industrial period when the main interest of hereditary monarchs was to impose tax and tariff on whatever money-making enterprise they could lay their hands on.

In the post-industrial period, however, it is proper that we lay to rest outdated quarrels with monarchs and use government as a social tool. An economy based on pure free market forces, with no government intervention, fails to come to grips with certain social and economic problems. The original assumption has been that a free market economy allows the interplay between producer and consumer to sort things out for the benefit of all. This is not always the case. Take the example of DDT. The chemical companies and the farmers were very happy with DDT. Ultimately, farmers might have become dissatisfied, as their farms succumbed to irreversible ecological damage. However, long before then, the long-term economic problems of DDT, not to mention the potential ecological disaster, were avoided by public intervention. Hence the importance of government as a major actor in the present economy – it is crucial for regulating economic forces which might go awry.

It is likely that at some point in the future many of the services provided by government will either no longer be required or alternatively will revert to the private sector. This tantalising possibility, the 'Coming Entrepreneurial Revolution', has been explored in depth by Norman Macrae, deputy editor of *The Economist*, in a series of articles in that journal (25 December 1976). Macrae considers that the era of the big business corporation is drawing to an end and that big business will not be displaced by state capitalism. Instead, Macrae envisions a whole host of small businesses operating at the local community level ranging from traditional manufacture (using advanced high-technology machine robots in backyard sheds) to community services including fire and police protection. Certainly there is no reason to assume that the institution of government will not continue to evolve, perhaps ultimately even disappear as did the institutions of absolute monarchy and slavery.

In maturing post-industrial economies one can already detect a reversal of the traditional trend, discussed above, from private industry to public utility. Both nuclear energy and communications satellites illustrate the principle of high-technology systems which were initially developed by the government, then transferred to private industry. This trend will probably increase as we move deeper into post-industrial economies. Early developments of major new technologies may require massive investments of high-risk capital. The uncertainties and long payback times discourage the private sector from attempting such ambitious ventures. The government, having both a secure financial base, and usually a non-economic motive as well, can justify such investments. The non-economic motives for the development of the nuclear and space technologies involved matters of defence and national prestige. They may also involve political, social or economic considerations. A contemporary case, using the government for regulating a critical resource, is exemplified by the Israeli government, a state whose land is subjected to arid or desert conditions. To the Israelis, 'Water

resources are public property, subject to the control of the state
...' The government not only builds, maintains and runs the
water grid system, but conducts research into increasing water
resources. In view of the high value of water in desert areas, it
is probable that private companies could also do very well, but
from the point of view of the well-being of all citizens, probably
not as well. The pressure to make profits would tend to reduce
investments with a long payback period, and it would certainly
not favour the marginal (usually poor) consumer. The Israeli
enterprise insures a more complete and stable infrastructure.

It is not only for regulating a critical resource such as water,
or developing a new one, such as electricity, that government
may become the instrument for creating a more equitable and
prosperous society. The state may also be used, in a broader
arena, as an instrument of economic policy. For example,
government fiscal policy is an attempt, if not always successful,
to steer the economy so as to achieve maximum happiness for
all.

GOVERNMENT AS INVESTOR

It is easy to see that when the government is busy building
roads, docks or airports, it is investing in the economy of the
country. Private enterprises can engage and have engaged in
such activities. However, such projects are often carried out
more effectively by the government. Building roads, docks and
airports helps provide a transport infrastructure which is a
prerequisite for running modern economies. One cannot run an
economy without these facilities. When the government builds
them, it is investing in the economy as a whole.

When the government builds post offices and telephone exchanges, it is investing in the physical aspects of a communications infrastructure. Likewise, when the government builds
sewage plants, lays down gas pipes, constructs electricity pylons
or digs reservoirs, it is busy investing in the economy. It is
engaged in activities which create the physical plant or equipment, the physical infrastructure, which makes a modern economy more productive.

What is more subtle is the intellectual infrastructure required to run an information economy. That base rests on the education system and on research and development. Without education, it would not be possible to have the many skills necessary – from operating a crane to managing a multinational company – for running a post-industrial economy. Government expenditures on education, therefore, must be classed as investment: education creates the intellectual infrastructure for both the knowledge industry and the myriad of information inputs into the other sectors of the economy.

Similar, and perhaps more obvious, is government expenditure on research and development. A good illustration is provided by the US agricultural sector, which is one of the most productive in the world. A great deal of this productivity is the result of government information inputs: the federal and state experiment stations, the special agricultural research centres, the colleges of agriculture and the universities, all carry out the research which leads to improved fertilisers and machinery, hybrid seeds and new lines of cattle, contour ploughing, insect and other pest control, new storage techniques and numerous other technological developments. County agents and the agricultural extension services speed the flow of information to the farmer. It is the county agent who keeps abreast of the new techniques and equipment which are of relevance to the farmers in his district. Finally, everyone, particularly the farmer himself, must be sufficiently educated to understand and apply this new information effectively. In all these ways the government provides or supports the intellectual infrastructure necessary for furnishing the information inputs into modern, technologised agriculture.

The government assured the profound rise in US agricultural productivity not only by providing the intellectual infrastructure, but also by providing much of the energy infrastructure. The Rural Electrification Administration (REA) was set up with the goal of electrifying every farm, thus speeding up farm modernisation.

Finally, beginning with the Hoover administration in 1929,

the Federal Farm Board was set up. A new era of direct aid to farmers began. The Farm Credit Administration was set up to let farmers borrow at low interest rates. By 1933 farm price legislation was introduced. Government price-fixing created stable prices for the farmers. This allowed them to invest in the equipment and technology required to increase output. At least part of the great increase in agricultural productivity dates back to the 1930s, as the government began to support the farmers and to provide them with a stable financial and market infrastructure, as well as a sound technical and educational base.

In the US by the late 1970s the total value of farm output was close to 6 per cent of the US gross national product, while it took substantially less than 3 per cent of the labour force to produce this. The great increases in productivity and the wealth-generating potential of agriculture must have derived largely from previous government investments.

GOVERNMENT AS CONSUMER

As we have seen, the money spent by government to support farmers (technically, financially and educationally) not only improves the farmers' condition, it also stimulates the economy as a whole. As a result, a much larger tax revenue returns to the government. For this reason much of the government's expenditure is clearly investment and must be classed as such. Yet, traditionally, government expenditures are classed as consumption. For example, the current convention in national income accounting also treats all health and education expenditures as consumption. This practice does not recognise the value of human capital as an integral part of the nation's wealth. In an information economy such an analysis is disastrous. Imagine the problems of ascertaining the GNP, or the national wealth, in an industrial society using criteria which recognise agriculture alone as being productive. Yet today we are in a very similar position. We seem to believe that only the production of goods represent wealth. How can we evaluate the GNP and the wealth of a nation in an information economy? Education adds value to human capital. If human capital is not part of the nation's wealth, then education is economically valueless. Until we get out from under the type of thinking that regards material wealth as the only wealth, we will fail to understand government expenditures on education as investment and instead mistake it for consumption. And we will be very puzzled as the education industry becomes the number one employer over the next few decades.

EXPANSION OF THE PUBLIC SERVICE SECTOR

In his general theory (*The General Theory of Employment Interest and Money*) Keynes describes the case in which an economy may reach equilibrium at a lower level of activity than its full potential. This means that the 'actual' gross national product (GNP) is substantially below the 'potential' GNP – the level at which production is close to maximum and employment close to 100 per cent. Keynes's monumental work was published in 1936. Within a decade a new orthodoxy had developed which stated that modern economies were subject to a deficiency in demand, and that government action was required to counterbalance the deflationary trends. Hitler and Roosevelt were among the first to use Keynesian doctrines (if not always consciously) to pull Germany and the US out of the Great Depression of the 1930s.

The idea that one must orient government spending to wealth creation may come hard to classical Keynesians. To them the limiting factor in modern economies is the level of consumption. In a stagnating economy the function of government is to stimulate consumption. In their strictest application Keynesian doctrines would accept as perfectly logical the government digging a ditch from one end of the country to the other and then filling it in again. The money spent by the government would end up as wages in the pockets of the ditch diggers and profits in the bank accounts of the contractors. These would stimulate further demand and investment, and the downward economic spiral would thus be reversed.

Monetarists, and other conservative opposition to Keynesian policies, objects to the inflation caused by this process. However, the analysis on which this opposition is based is usually wrong. The main concern relates to government deficit spending, i.e. that the government spends more than it takes in. This is the wrong focus. Even if the books balance, unproductive spending leads to inflation. Unproductive spending stimulates demand without increasing production. Unproductive spending stresses limited resources such as land, labour, capital, energy, materials or specific items such as oil, spare parts, ditch diggers or skilled engineers. Whatever the limiting factors may be, a further demand on them will cause a rise in price. The classic example is oil in the 1970s. Between 1970 and 1976 the price of oil increased from \$US1.80 to \$US11.25 per barrel; by 1980 it had climbed to well over \$US30. Such a rise in the price of oil inevitably brought about a rise in the prices of virtually all commodities. The increased costs of oil imports resulted in a combination of decreased living standards (deflationary forces) or increased debt (inflationary forces). Thus the economists were confronted by a new situation – 'stagflation', i.e. the simultaneous appearance of economic stagnation and inflation.

The only way effectively to counter this increase in oil price, without incurring either a recession or inflation, was either to improve the productivity per unit of oil consumed, or develop a substitute for oil which will provide the same quantity of energy, or valuable chemicals, at the old price. Another option would be to earn more money elsewhere, allowing the extra income to pay for the increase in oil prices.

The national arguments should not be the one-dimensional argument between Keynesians who want to get out of a recession by digging a ditch, and monetarists who do not want to spend government money for fear of inflation. As Samuel Brittan has pointed out, governments can exhibit high levels of spending yet retain stable prices. 'Economists who have tried to find a historical link between public spending (as distinct from borrowing) and inflation have not been very successful.' Political decisions should be based on the most sensible way for a government to spend money both to get out of a recession and to avoid inflation. If digging a ditch makes no sense, building the Severn Barrage does. Both create jobs and stimulate the economy. However, the former yields no economic return but the latter provides electricity from a renewable energy source which, in turn, pays the government back its investment. Most defence spending provides no economic return. Nor does putting people on the dole. In an energy-hungry economy is it better to put people in the army (as Hitler did) or put them to work building wave-power devices? We will look at these questions again in greater detail in later chapters.

What is crucial to the argument here is the understanding that government must be treated as a form of social and economic technology which, like any other technology, needs to be used imaginatively. The neo-Keynesian/monetarist dialogue is largely irrelevant to post-industrial economies. The focus must be on government schemes to create new sources of wealth. Like North Sea oil, the world is full of 'non-resources' waiting to be converted to revenue-yielding resources. With rising unemployment it makes no sense to wait for private enterprise to develop each scheme entirely on its own.

To sum up, this chapter began by examining Adam Smith's attitude to government and then reviewed some of the contemporary attitudes towards government. Government was considered as a service provider, as a form of social technology, as an investor, and as a consumer. The tendency for traditional economists is to class government as a consumer. This leads to the assumption that all forms of public service sector spending are inflationary. In fact there is no correlation between inflation and high levels of government spending (in contrast to borrowing). The key is to differentiate between productive spending, which yields as return on investment, and consumptive spending, which does not.

In the past many private enterprises evolved into public sector enterprises (e.g. turnpikes, postal services and education). In the future public enterprises, directly and indirectly, will create private enterprises. This has already begun in high-technology areas such as computers, nuclear energy and space technology. The imaginative use of government spending can successfully counteract inflation and recession at the same time. Let there develop a vigorous public service sector of the economy whose main function is to invest, research, develop and act as powerful economic pioneer.

7 Shifting employment patterns and the new technology

'In consequence of better machinery, of greater dexterity, and of a more proper division and distribution of work, all of which are the natural effects of improvement, a much smaller quantity of labour becomes requisite for executing any particular piece of work . . .'

Adam Smith, Book One, Chapter XI.

There are two major components to unemployment. The first is cyclic, the second structural. The cyclic phenomenon relates to the general economic activity; that is to say, when times are good there is a marked expansion of activities, whether in the service sector or in the manufacturing sector, which is reflected in the number of job vacancies. When times go bad the reverse is true.

The structural component invariably represents advances in technology affecting labour requirements directly or indirectly. First, technology (that is, knowing how to do things) diffuses to other countries. Such countries stop being customers and then, as a result of the availability of cheap transport and effective communications, may actually turn around and become competitors. The second process involves a reduction in demand for an existing product because it has become outdated. The use of valves for radios decreased as they were displaced by the transistor. The third involves the direct displacement of labour by improvements in machinery or organisation. These processes show in the unemployment curves of certain western countries since the mid-1960s as a 'ratchet effect'. Unemployment peaks up during recessions, then drops again as times get better – but not to its previous low. This higher level is then the base line for the next recession, which produces a higher peak than the previous one, only to drop again as business picks up again, but not to its previous level etc.

This process is illustrated in the 1966–81 unemployment curves for the US and the UK (see fig. 7.1 reproduced courtesy of the

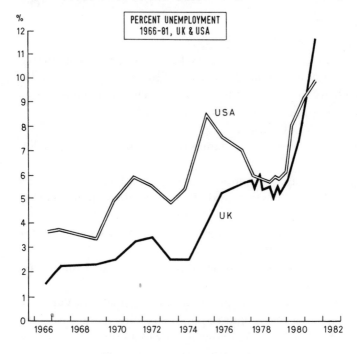

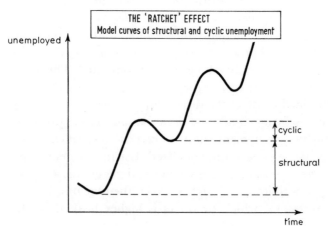

Financial Times). For the UK the Thatcher peak of 1980 exceeded the Callaghan peak of 1978, which exceeded the Heath peak of 1972, which in turn exceeded the Wilson plateau of the late 1960s. The rise and fall of unemployment represents the cyclic component. The differences between two low points (rather than the peaks) probably represents the structural component. The difference consists of that part of the labour force which is not being reabsorbed into the economy as business gets better. The employment opportunities have simply disappeared. Only with time, as whole new employment sectors open up (e.g. the public service sector), does such structural unemployment disappear. The ratchet effect is a reflection of the shift into a post-industrial economy and will continue to worsen until the economy finally reaches a new equilibrium as an information economy rather than as a transition state.

SHIFT TO OTHER COUNTRIES

The shift of an industry or service to other countries is a historical process involving the maturation of industries, such as textiles, steel, shipbuilding, heavy engineering and automobiles. As these industries matured, the knowledge of how to create and run them transferred to other parts of the world. In due course former customers no longer required these products or services and after a while became competitors. This process was accelerated, particularly in those industries in which labour costs increased rapidly, because there was a distinct advantage to moving into countries where labour was cheaper. In 1981 Coats Patons, a major British manufacturing group, released the figures which represented this multinational's calculation on its relative labour costs (*Financial Times*, 29 June 1981). In 1979 it had a £989 million turnover with more than 90 per cent of the group's trading profits coming from overseas. Using a mix of factors such as exchange rates, base wages and extra charges on labour such as national insurance, there emerged the following comparisons of this company's own perception of its own labour force: if the UK's total labour cost per hour worked on a single shift is pegged at 100, then comparable costs

in the US would be at 117, Italy 122, West Germany 133 and
Canada at 134. Contrast this with Portugal's 40, Columbia at
36, Brazil at 31, Peru at 23, India at 13, the Philippines at 10
and Indonesia at 6. It becomes apparent why there is such a
great pressure to move operations to Third World countries. In
1980, as the west European steel industry was undergoing dras-
tic cutbacks, the steel industry was thriving in parts of the Third
World such as Latin America and Asia. Output in these Third
World countries was growing at rates exceeding 10 per cent per
year. Nor were these countries merely supplying cheap labour.
For example, new technology coupled with cheap energy, in
the form of natural gas, favoured the production of directly
reduced iron (DRI) in Mexico, Venezuela and Indonesia. The
DRI was then shipped to European steelmakers, as well as local
steel mills, for feedstock. The combination of cheap labour,
cheap energy and new technology increasingly gave Third
World countries a 'comparative' advantage, making the European steel industry increasingly redundant.

There is a second group of countries often overlooked in this
process because of a scarcity of hard information: countries with
state-run economies which can deflate wages artificially. Not
only do Comecon countries produce a lot of steel, but increasingly all kinds of manufactured goods ranging from textiles to
automobiles – goods which can be sold more cheaply because of
the controlled economy, including the 'comparative advantage'
accruing from cheap labour coupled with increasingly sophisticated technology. This process does not confine itself to manufacturing. By the end of the 1970s, in the quest for foreign
exchange in the form of hard western currency, the Russians
had taken to maritime transport with a vengeance. By using
naval conscripts to fulfil their national service requirements as
sailors and officers on a fleet of modern cargo carriers, the
Russians had developed an effective combination of cheap
labour and advanced technology. Coupled with an accounting
system more interested in earning foreign exchange than clearing a large profit, Soviet tenders frequently underbid traditional
shippers and picked up the trade.

The matter of labour inputs is crucial for understanding the shift of mature industries from the West to either the socialist bloc countries or, particularly, the Third World. Non-western (OECD) labour inputs have an advantage in both the price and sometimes the quality of the labour input – the ability and willingness to carry out tasks. It is clear that in poverty-stricken countries where jobs are at a premium, people are willing to work under conditions or for periods of time not acceptable to their western counterparts. Furthermore, the political situation in many of these countries does not favour the development of strong trade unions, therefore industrial discipline can be maintained with greater ease. Undesirable as this situation is for workers both in Third World countries and in the West, it would be unrealistic not to state this as one of the major causes for industries moving to Third World countries.

This movement must be studied in the broader social context because there are distinct benefits. First of all, in many parts of the world, having a hard and low-paid job is better than having no job at all. Second, and more significant, there are a number of Third World countries which are beginning to reduce the gap between the rich and the poor countries. A survey conducted by Michael Beenstock and Patrick Willcocks of the London Business School, looking at the United Nations' statistics, has shown that a number of less developed countries have increased their industrial productivity remarkably. Their studies indicate that, contrary to popular opinion, the Third World as a whole is reducing the gap, at least in terms of industrial production and of GDP. And the authors attribute this directly to the comparative advantage these countries have. The authors also attribute the unemployment problems in the West, at least in part, to this shift.

This process of shifting the comparative advantage to newly industrialised countries has been going on for many decades, particularly in textiles. It has been said that there were never as many cotton mills built in the Manchester area as around 1919, after the end of World War I. Most of those mills never made it. The reason for the massive expansion was the view that, with

the war over, business was back to normal. Since business had
been booming earlier in the century, so it would again. All those
customers, for example India, which had been deprived of
cotton goods during the war years would now constitute an
enormous market which needed filling. Instead what had happened was that the Indians, in the absence of available textiles
from England, had started to develop their own textile industry.
Thus India became not only a non-customer but a competitor.

Unlike textiles, textile machinery went into a boom following
World War I. In 1922 the value of all textile machinery exported more than doubled the value of any pre-war year. Taking exports to India as an example, the value of the imports of
cotton textile machinery into India during the 1917–20 period
declined to about a third of its pre-war level. (During the war
years, Japan began to pick up some orders; and, for a brief
period following the war, so did the United States.)

However, once the British engineering industry had completed its return to peace-time operations, it had no trouble in
recapturing this market so that by 1922 it accounted for over 98
per cent of India's imports. Thus British exports to India had
shifted from exporting textiles to exporting textile machinery.
This is a typical example of technology diffusing to a Third
World country.

Once started, cheap labour coupled with modern machinery
created products sufficiently cheap to be exported back into the
original country, threatening even the domestic markets. Every
major industry which developed in the West in due course, as it
matured, migrated to other parts of the world. The process
continues. For example, the mature industries in Japan are
migrating, or have migrated, to what Johan Galtung calls little
Japans: Korea, Taiwan, Hong Kong and Singapore.

By now the migration of industries to Third World and
Comecon countries is well recognised. But what, or who, is next?
One obvious candidate is base petrochemicals. There exists a
large capacity to produce these substances in the western world
– a capacity sufficient to cause serious friction between the US
and western Europe during times of recession (such as the late

1970s and early 1980s). Added to this is the growing capability in Comecon countries. However, the real problems for the western petrochemicals industry will come as oil-rich countries get into the game. By 1980 several of these OPEC countries had either contracted, or were negotiating, for a variety of petrochemical projects. For example, the Shell group and Saudi Basic Industries Corporation were planning for a $US3 billion complex on Saudi Arabia's east coast to use methane and ethane as raw material to produce 650,000 tonnes/year of ethylene plus large quantities of styrene, ethylene dichloride, ethanol and caustic soda. What is so significant about this venture is that the methane and ethane were 'useless' by-products of the oil fields, simply flared off. Therefore one could invoke one kind of accounting which would ascribe zero cost to some of the raw material. Even with higher labour costs, financing costs will be lower and raw material costs will be close to zero. The comparative advantage to the Saudis will be enormous ...

Such agreements are not confined to Shell. A $US1.6 billion agreement with Mobil for another large ethylene plant on the Red Sea was signed in March 1980. This plant is scheduled to produce other base chemicals as well, including low-density polyethylene and ethylene glycol. Other planned ventures include a similar type petrochemical complex involving now a $US2 billion deal with Exxon; a $US268 million methanol plant with a Japanese consortium; and a $US376 million ammonia/urea joint scheme with the Taiwan Fertilizer Company. The Arab countries are greatly aided by the advances in transport technology which now make it possible to ship cheaply dangerous chemicals such as ammonia and methane.

Countries lacking a comparative advantage in cheap labour, capital, energy or raw materials, or more probably a combination of these, may not survive into the 1990s. There is, however, one kind of advantage – information advantage – know-how – which would allow industries in the western petrochemical industry to survive and perhaps even expand: that is, to move technologically upstream, away from base chemicals into specialised items such as agrochemicals (including single-cell protein), pharmaceuticals, special plastics or mixed materials (plastics plus ceramics). Nevertheless, they must begin an orderly retreat, or else it may end up as a complete rout, as did the steel industry.

OUTDATED INDUSTRIES

The second major reason for the creation of structural un-employment within an industry is that jobs are lost simply because an industry or service is no longer needed. Scribes disappeared as virtually everybody learned to read and write. Coopers disappeared as barrel production shifted to mechanised technology. Factories producing mechanical adding machines and cash registers closed because such machines simply could not compete with advanced electronic devices.

THE DISPLACEMENT OF LABOUR

The third form of structural unemployment involves the steady displacement of labour as technology in all its manifestations continues to advance. Technology, it must be remembered, includes not only specific items of hardware but also other scientific breakthroughs, new forms of doing things, new organ-isational structures and new institutional structures. A good illustration of a combination of physical and organisational technology displacing labour is illustrated by the Port of New York, which moved into containerisation in the late 1960s. In 1968 the port employed about 24,000 dockers who worked a total of 44 million hours that year. By 1979 the workforce had shrunk to 11,000 dockers, putting in fewer hours each (for a total of 18 million work hours), even though the port was booming and handling over twice the volume of 1968. By 1980 only 6,500 of those 11,000 were actually needed for work. The other 4,500 were operating on the Guaranteed Annual Income (GAI) scheme negotiated by the union which means that they checked in every morning, waited for assignments, then went home for lack of work – but were still paid a day's wages. This may beat putting workers on the dole but in the long run there must be more efficient ways of solving the problem.

A highly mechanised port such as New York can handle cargo much faster than ports lacking comparable facilities. Time spent loading and unloading a ship costs money. Not only must the shipper pay dock charges and wages, but the ship is uselessly tied up when it might be on the high seas delivering its next load. Therefore a modern port such as New York picks up a good deal of business which might, in earlier times, have gone elsewhere. Advanced technology is good for business; it is also good for those workers employed in high-technology industries (New York dockers in 1980, including those on GAI, were paid in excess of $13 an hour). Advanced technology is usually not good for general levels of employment. However, the opposite, a lack of up-to-date technology, becomes disastrous for everybody: uncompetitive facilities or organisations go broke.

The 'good times/bad times' paradigm combines the cyclic and structural components of unemployment. Envisage a company such as a steel corporation. Assume that it is receiving a lot of orders in some specific category which it cannot fill. The company decides to expand production by building a new plant. The increase in the cost of constructing an advanced production plant is only about 5 per cent more than building a conventional one. The incentive is great to spend the extra money – new technology allows one to do things one could not do before (usually this is the primary motivation when new technology first becomes available), and one saves on labour. The latter means increased productivity and competitive advantage. Because it is a new plant, trade union involvement tends to be positive. There is no objection from any of the participants. The matter is viewed as good for the industry, therefore good for the workforce as well, even though the new plant may require only 30 per cent of the labour force for a comparable output. Let's say it employs 3,000 people but they are now able, by virtue of the new technology, to produce as much as 10,000 workers do in an older plant. The company involved is delighted: orders are being filled, there is a substantial profit and there is a significant increase in productivity. The workforce is happy because it involves 3,000 new jobs and because, in a new plant, the working conditions are probably better. Furthermore salaries and wages may be higher. Everybody is happy.

Things work very nicely until bad times. There is a recession or for some other reason there is a decline in orders. The company faced with financial losses is put in a position where it cannot possibly justify running two plants except as a matter of public charity. In fact, if it is a large industry, and especially if it is a government-run corporation, enormous political pressure is brought to bear to put public funds into the company to keep it going. One can cite innumerable cases in the western world where public funds have been used to support an obsolete industrial structure because of the large number of jobs involved. Anyway, a point comes where the economic pressure becomes overwhelming and a decision is made to close one of the two plants. Question: which plant is going to be closed? The highly productive modern one, or the less productive traditional one which, by world standards, is now obsolete? The answer is obvious. The older plant is shut down and 10,000 workers are put on the dole.

After a while, if the company survived, business picks up again. The question facing management is: if you want to increase production again do you do it by reopening an obsolete plant? Obviously the answer tends to be no; you either modernise the plant so that now you need only 5,000 workers or, more likely, you go somewhere else and open a plant that is even more modern than the one you opened up a few years ago – this one only needs 2,000 workers. As the plant opens, the headlines say, 'XYZ Corporation Opens New Plant – 2,000 Jobs' and everybody's feeling is 'Ah ha! here's the beginning of the job recovery.' In fact those 2,000 workers now produce as much as the 10,000 did before and unless it is a rapidly expanding market, and five plants are built instead of one, it means that 8,000 jobs are lost to the industry.

This then is the explanation of the ratchet effect. In bad times labour-intensive, low-productivity operations are most likely to be closed, while in good times technologically advanced, high-productivity systems are introduced. Thus there appears a wave of unemployed workers during a recession of which only a relatively small proportion may be reabsorbed as times improve. Note that in this process no one is directly displaced by technology – yet advancing technology is the root cause of the rising unemployment.

This mechanism can occur within a single company or industry, or it can happen across industries within a country, or it can happen transnationally. Within the UK British Steel opened up a new complex at Redcar and not long after closed down Schotten; as the technologically advanced coalfields of Selby began producing, older mines in Wales and South Yorkshire began to shut; as telecommunications advanced, mail deliveries declined. As long as there is a substantial demand, the economy can carry the less efficient operations. Once a recession sets in and demand declines, the inefficient producers fall by the wayside.

STEADY TECHNOLOGICAL PRESSURE

There is another process by which technology displaces labour: the 'steady technological pressure' paradigm illustrated by a large printing plant in West Yorkshire. In one corner of this printing plant 1907 linotype equipment was still being used on occasion in the late 1970s, while at the opposite corner were advanced word-processors coupled with automated equipment. The policy agreed with the trade union was this: the company was allowed to introduce new equipment providing no one was made redundant. Therefore, as new equipment was brought in, the company would retrain some of the workers to handle the new equipment.

It turned out to be a satisfactory scheme. Management was able to introduce new equipment which allowed it to carry out tasks which it was often unable to perform previously. Productivity increased. The workforce was happy because no one was dismissed. One of their members was trained on a new and often exciting piece of equipment and, in addition, was likely to get some increase in wages. The trade union was happy because the workers were happy. Management was happy because they had acquired both new equipment and good industrial relations. Everyone was happy. Just one problem: they hired almost no one over a long time.

The people who were not hired, of course, were the young entering the labour market. This is the major reason why a disproportionate part of the unemployed are young people, particularly those who come out of an education system which was designed to fill the lower unskilled and semi-skilled echelons of productive enterprises. These young people are wholly un-equipped to enter a post-industrial economy.

It is a long-term problem. Nowhere is this more apparent than in the agricultural sector. About 300 years ago it took over 90 per cent of the labour force to work on farms in order to feed

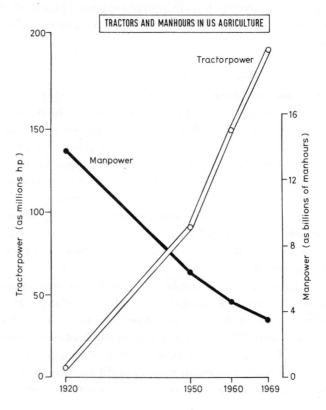

the other 10 per cent and themselves. Today, in technologically advanced countries, and in particular in the United States, it takes well below 3 per cent of the workforce to work on farms not only to feed the other 97 per cent of Americans, but to provide food for much of the rest of humanity as well. The shift in technology and labour patterns can be summarised by fig. 7.2 which uses as an indicator of technologisation of farms the number of millions of horsepower of tractors in operation (that is, to say either more tractors or bigger tractors) and compares these with the labour used in the system. One can see from the figure that there is a close correlation between reduction in work hours and increase in tractor horsepower. Tractors did not displace people – they displaced horses. But coming with the tractors were new fertilisers, insecticides, hybrid seeds, hybrid cattle, weather forecasts and financial stability, either through government subsidy or contracting with large firms or grain speculators. It was the combination of new organisation and institutional structuring, as well as new technology, including the increasing use of energy, which fostered this reduction in farm labour requirements.

The decline in numbers of farm workers in the US during this century is illustrated in fig. 7.3. Farm labour reached its peak in absolute numbers around World War I, then declined steadily. By 1980 fewer people were living on farms in the US than back in 1830 – farm labour had shrunk to about 2.5 per cent of the US labour force.

In the late 1970s US employment in manufacture and direct services levelled. By the early 1980s the decline in absolute numbers will become apparent. What happened to the farm workers will happen to workers in these areas. The percentage of the labour force working in US manufacturing has been declining since the 1950s as these workers are being overtaken by service and, in particular, information operatives.

Information operatives are those who make a living working with information, i.e. creating, transmitting, organising, storing and retrieving or receiving it. Their tools generally are a pen and the telephone, or equivalent devices, which allow them to

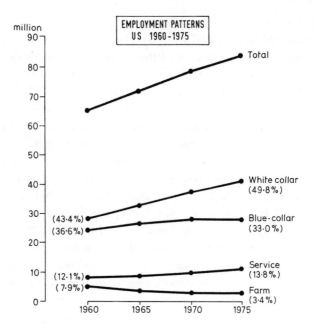

store, transcribe or communicate information. Their ranks include scientists, professionals, educators, managers, technical salesmen, typists, filing clerks and students. They comprise the dominant form of labour in the post-industrial economy.

BRADFORD: A CASE STUDY

Bradford in West Yorkshire is the former 'Wool Capital of the World'. It is a classic example of a city which owed its existence to the Industrial Revolution and the industrial economy. From a sleepy village of a few thousand in 1800 it grew to over 100,000 by 1850 and about 150,000 by the mid-1870s. Its prosperity was based on a combination of fortuitous local environmental and cultural resources. West Yorkshire had a long tradition of sheep-raising and wool textiles. As the Industrial Revolution spread across the north of England, Bradford found plenty of local coal and water to drive its textile machinery with steam. It also possessed a second type of coal, good for making coke, which, when combined with local iron, laid the foundation for its engineering industries. Connecting Bradford with the Leeds–Liverpool Canal and later the railway network opened it to the rest of Britain, then the world. The result: a city of almost unprecedented prosperity by late Victorian times.

Bradford grew as labour was shifting from farm to factory. Bradford experienced all the worst features of the Industrial Revolution. The pall of industrial smoke hung so heavily over the city that it has been said that a whole century elapsed before people in some parts of the city could see the other side of the valley. Life expectancy at birth in the early days of the city was 18.7 years. By far more people died in the city than were born there, yet they kept coming. Each year the city grew by 5 per cent.

Bradford suffered the technological shocks which swept the textile industry. As the mill-owners switched to steam-powered looms in the late 1820s thousands of hand-loom weavers were thrown out of work. Other skilled textile workers were overtaken by the same fate – the last to go were the wool-combers. All the filth and grime, disease, injustice and greed were there; and yet, in cycles of growth and depression, it kept growing and prospering. By late Victorian times foreign competition, mainly from Europe and the US, forced slowing and final stagnation. By World War I the iron had run out and engineering began to decline. Textiles, and associated industries such as dyeing, wool-sorting and textile machinery, although they had their ups and downs, remained reasonably strong. Some specialised engineering works such as the Jowett car plant (later taken over by International Harvester) and, during World War II, the introduction of an expanding electronics industry, maintained the essentially industrial nature of the city.

Yet by 1975 this bastion of the Industrial Revolution had capitulated. Textile workers had lost their status as the dominant category of labour – they had slipped to the second position. The dominant category came under the heading of 'professional and scientific services'. Bradford University, established in 1967, had become one of the biggest employers, while the major employer was the Bradford Corporation itself, the local city government!

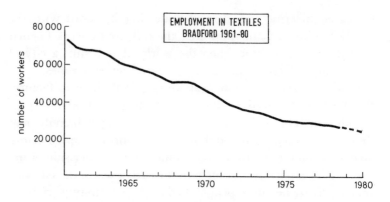

The fate of Bradford's textile workers during the 1960s and 1970s is depicted in figure 7.4. Their total of about 70,000 in 1961 was cut in half over the next two decades. During the 1970s the decline of industrial employment accelerated. Between 1976 and 1980 there occurred a 30 per cent decline in the workforce of the ten largest manufacturers – from 17,000 to 12,000. One of these firms, Thorn Consumer Electronics, which in 1973 boasted the largest television factory in Europe, and which at peak production, in 1974, produced over 10,000 sets per week while employing 4,700 workers, closed completely in 1978 with a loss of over 2,000 jobs. Another, Associated Weavers, employed 2,500 people in 1976 which dropped to 1,600 by 1979, and over half of these were being made redundant in 1980. International Harvester closed its operations in 1982.

It should be stressed that output declined much less dramatically. Highly productive operations, especially those which cornered a specialist share of the market, continued to do well financially. However, the labour inputs continued to decline. Thus structural unemployment had begun to settle on Bradford with an official rate of 6.8 per cent by 1980 and an increasing number of 'hard-core' unemployed. Nearly a quarter of the 13,500 officially unemployed had been looking for work for over a year. In addition to the officially unemployed there were several other categories of people out of work. These included married women (who do not show up on the unemployment rolls), people who retired early and young people in special job-creation programmes.

Two other indicators of structural unemployment included the reduction in engineering apprenticeships, which were expected (a fall of 30 per cent in 1980), and the rising unemployment in Bradford's Asian community. A large section of the Asian labour force tended to be concentrated in the manufacturing industries. For example, they accounted for 20 per cent of the textile workers. When Thorn's electronic plant closed, the redundant workers were mainly Asian women. Since they were predominantly low-skilled workers, it is not surprising that eight months after closure less than half had found alternative work. Nor is it surprising that by 1980 unemployment among Asian workers had risen to twice their proportion in the labour force.

In contrast to the employment pattern in manufacturing, in Bradford's service sector the ten largest employers had increased their workforce by 1,500, continuing the transition from manufacturing to services which had overtaken the city by the mid-1970s. Thus the fate of the Wool Capital of the World . . .

INFORMATION DEVICES

The whole pace of invention has accelerated to the point where it changes all aspects of society. Among the more dramatic of the recent advances in the technology of information devices is the micro-processor.

The piano roll serves as a model for understanding what modern information devices do in various industrial and commercial production processes. A piano roll allows a piano to play in the absence of a pianist. Similarly there is emerging a whole series of devices now which allow a drill press to drill in the absence of an operator, a word-processor to type a standard letter in the absence of a typist, or a cash dispenser to provide money in the absence of a bank teller.

Until the arrival of the micro-processor computers were too expensive to couple with these various machines. People were cheaper. However, the techniques for making silicon chips have become so advanced that it is now possible to produce such micro-processors for well below a dollar.

The price of computers has dropped 10,000 fold over a thirty-year period. At the same time the micro-processor of today has far more computing capacity than the world's first large electronic computer, ENIAC. The micro-processor operates very much faster, has a larger memory, is a thousand times more reliable and consumes the power of a tiny light bulb rather than that of a locomotive. It occupies an incredibly tiny bit of space. Over a forty-year period the computer has evolved from a device which would occupy a large hall belonging to a large corporation or government department to a device which may be installed inside an average householder's light switch.

THE ROBOTS ARE COMING!

The rate at which a new technology spreads is a direct function of its advantage (price, capability, reliability, durability and capacity). The steam locomotive, for example, spread rather slowly in the early nineteenth century because at that stage it did not provide a great advantage over horses. In fact, some historians believe that following the Napoleonic wars had the price of oats dropped to its pre-war level, steam locomotives would not have appeared for another several decades. Contrast the spread of locomotives, in the early nineteenth century, with the spread of antibiotics or transistor radios in the middle of the twentieth. Once the product became reliable and cheap enough, it took less than a decade for the technology to become firmly rooted around the world.

People have been predicting for some time that computers would displace people from jobs, that they would cause horrific unemployment. These forecasts were essentially correct although the timescale was wrong. Technological forecasts frequently fall into two kinds of traps. Technologists making forecasts may become so enamoured of achievements and possibilities that they mistake technological potential for economic reality. At the other extreme are economists whose forecasts are based on past performance, and on technology as it is practised at the moment, but who fail to appreciate how far a new (but not widely used) technology may have progressed and who have no comprehension of its potential.

The rate at which a new technology displaces old technology depends on how much better it is. It may involve other factors but price is often crucial. Coupling micro-processors now with either a drill press or a typewriter makes it cheaper to operate than when it is coupled with a human operator. The machines can work twenty-four hours a day, 365 days a year; they do not take time for tea breaks; they do not complain if they are idle for six months because production does not require them; they never go on strike; they never report sick (unless they are badly designed); and now they cost less than three years' wages. We are beginning to see assembly lines in a number of manufacturing processes where there is virtually no human being in sight. What sort of industrial robots are needed on assembly lines?

Let us begin with a spot welding machine. An advanced welding robot is instructed by having the best welder available taking the machine and repeating the exact movements that the welder would do as, let us say, a car is coming down the assembly line. The robot has a switch turned on at the control panel which signifies that it is now being instructed, and the robot will put into the associated memory of the micro-processor the exact movements of the operator. At the end of the instruction period the switch is turned to 'Operation'. The robot needs to be shown only once; it is the perfect apprentice. It will now repeat the operations as instructed with much greater precision than a human being could. It is probably faster and more reliable as well.

However, it is a rather stupid robot, and if the car is not lined up properly, it would just as soon weld the wing to the window as it would in the right place. For this reason, you put into the assembly line a series of monitoring robots which make sure that everything is lined up properly. They will either correct any faults or stop the system and alert the attending engineer that something is amiss – and very often exactly what is amiss.

In addition you can have robots controlling the assembly line overall and you can have robots keeping track of stocks as they are being used in the production process. Such robots can be instructed to report to the office the depletion of any stocks. Before long it should be possible to attach the terminals reporting such needs directly to the supplier. Why bother with the office?

Similarly, at the other end of the assembly line, you can have robots keeping track of the cars produced. These robots, too, could report to the office. But again, why bother? Why not have their terminals connected to the retailers all round the world, the way airlines have terminals connected to travel agents all over the world? That way, instead of making a large number of cars to wait on a parking lot, the retailers could simply communicate to the factory directly and communicate not only that they want a car, but they could communicate many individual details. Suppose someone wants a Mini painted in purple with two wing mirrors. There is no reason why that information could not be telexed to the head robot, who then activates the appropriate assembly line robots, the paint sprayer and the accessory-fitting robots to provide just what is wanted. Thus the robots will begin to displace not only workers on the shop floor but also some of the managers.

The same thing is going to happen increasingly in offices. Word-processors are being deployed now and they will greatly reduce the need for typists. Some time late in the 1980s there will appear the first voice-print machines. These are devices which translate the human spoken word into typed words. Coupled with personal computers, a manager could dictate a letter at home to a word-processor, edit it, then send the completed memo or letter electronically through the telephone to a colleague within the organisation or across the world ...

A META-TECHNOLOGY

The micro-processors and the micro-electronic technology constitute a new 'meta-technology'. The classic example is the steam engine. Initially invented to pump water out of mines it subsequently gave rise to a class of power machines which could be coupled with most other existing mechanical devices. The Industrial Revolution involved the spread of that meta-technology: coupling steam engines with all kinds of devices such as waggons (thereby creating locomotives), or weaving looms (thereby creating power looms). The displacement of labour during this process was horrific at times. In Bradford, as a result of the introduction of the power looms, about 10,000 hand-loom weavers were reduced to paupers around 1830.

The micro-processors comprise the new meta-technology: they are information machines which can convert existing machinery into 'smart' machinery which no longer needs human operators to guide it.

New machinery and devices are brought into established production processes because manufacturers want to reduce production costs by reducing the amount of labour required and want to avoid restrictions on production by labour which is either unable or unwilling to carry out the tasks. Finally, the new technology can achieve results which are impossible by human efforts alone. Machines can work under inhuman conditions. There can be no question that the 1980s are going to see a severe dislocation in employment patterns as the new micro-electronic technology begins to bite.

It is difficult to get precise figures and statements because employers are reluctant to discuss the introduction of new automated equipment for fear of precipitating crises with their local trade unions. This is less true within the computer industry itself and also perhaps in the electronics industry. Texas Instruments has about 75 per cent of its pocket calculator assembly line automated. In television manufacture most of the manual labour has been eliminated by automatic sequences, automatic insertion of components in printed circuit boards, wave soldering equipment and computer-controlled automatic test equipment. A single machine can insert components into a printed circuit board at the rate of 72,000 pieces an hour. It would require 240 workers to achieve that rate, yet the automatic insertion machines can be operated by as few as eleven workers. Not only does an automated process of this sort save labour; it also reduces the number of rejects, upgrades quality and reduces maintenance cost. This is why manufactured goods produced by advanced technology are both better in quality and cheaper in price than the manual-labour products of competitors.

The advances in information technology now permit the running of an entire complex industrial plant based on the concepts of decentralised control, distributed data acquisition and distributed information processing. This is a technical way of saying that instead of trying to run a whole plant by means of a single large computer, you run the various operations by means of individual micro-computers. These are hooked up through a communications network to control computers, which in turn are lined via another network to master computers. Thus a hierarchy is created of independent but interrelated activating, monitoring and adjusting devices much closer to the way a plant is run by human labour. This proves to be a much more versatile and reliable system. The first steel mill to operate on this principle is the Kimitsu Works of the Nippon Steel Company.

The use of multiple sensing devices and three-tier computer control system was actually pioneered by British Steel in the early 1970s. At its Scunthorpe works it developed a bloom and billet mill in which a crew of ten could put through 600 tons of steel an hour. In this mill the steel workers sit in air-conditioned control rooms above the molten ingots operating a few knobs and switches. Their main problem now is loneliness and boredom. This mill, with a capacity for converting 3 million ingot tons per year, demonstrates several important points. First, contrary to myth, British technology is not always behind, but may lead. Second, less parochially, this mill built in the early 1970s indicates how mature the automation technology is. This mill installed computer systems very much more expensive and less advanced than those available a decade later. Even so, the cost of the automated equipment was less than 5 per cent of the total construction costs: the entire mill cost about £58 million (at 1970 prices), while the computers and ancillary equipment cost about £2.3 million. Third, and rather sadly, the mill never ran at full capacity and now is beginning to feel the pinch of technological old age (having lost, as it were, its bloom). Not only are there further advances in computer technology, but steelmaking itself continues to change.

It is not only the computer technology, or micro-electronics, but all forms of technology whose progress is accelerating. However, in the 1980s much of the technological drama will centre on the micro-processor. Think of two earlier examples of non-automated technological displacement of labour: farm tractors and containerised transport. In the 1980s both will become automated. Think of the further increases in productivity as automated tractors work the fields during the night while the farmer sleeps. Automated crop sprayers use radar to detect wind changes and other factors to regulate droplet size, controlling pressure of application to maximise uniformity and minimise waste. Such equipment is commercially available now.

Even more dramatic is the Silocont system being developed for containerised ports. In this system automated cranes, able to identify individual containers and their destination, would be able to load and unload an entire freighter. Ultimately no workers would be needed at all, only supervisory engineers to make certain that everything was running smoothly. The entire Port of New York might be run by a few hundred docker/engineers.

Micro-electronics will not only have an impact on transportation but obviously on communications as well. The British Post Office will introduce its System X telephone equipment in the 1980s. Not only will it ultimately require only 4 per cent of the workforce needed to build the current, electro-mechanical Strowger, but once it is installed the new equipment will require hardly any maintenance. The Post Office has also begun to install its computer-based Prestel information-communications system, which will obviate the need for many intermediaries. In the long run one would expect the vast bulk of real estate, travel, employment and ticket agents, and similar services, to become greatly reduced.

Coupling the computer with a money-counting machine creates an automatic cash point. Cash-dispensing machines first

appeared in the 1960s as a source of money outside banking
hours. By the late 1970s, even though they were still fairly
expensive machines, they had evolved into an all-hours, all-
purpose substitute for bank tellers. New technological improvements and a reduction in the costs of the machines are bound to
spread the automatic teller machines (ATMs) to every major
shopping area, railway station, airport and factory. Again the
use of computerised checkouts in supermarkets and stock-room
controls will greatly reduce the number of unskilled and semi-
skilled service jobs available in the retail trades, just we have
witnessed the decline of the petrol pump attendant. Last, the
numbers of office jobs are rapidly shrinking. Not only have
computers replaced hordes of payroll clerks, and the Xerox
machine has replaced rooms full of copy-typists, but now the
word-processors have entered the market. For example, in the
Bradford local government, one department introduced such a
word-processor system into its typing pool. As a result the
workforce of 44 women was reduced to 22 (the rest being re-
deployed). This was accomplished with an overall productivity
increase claimed to be 30 per cent and an annual saving to the
city of £60,000. Also not to be overlooked is the fact that
whereas personnel turnover rates in the pool amounted to 30
per cent the previous year, it dropped to zero once the system
was installed. The women probably preferred working with the
new equipment.

   In 25 years it will take no more than 10 per cent of the labour
force to provide us with all our material needs. In post-industrial
society at present, it requires only a few per cent of the labour
force to work on farms and in the extractive industries. Less
than a third of the labour force is engaged in manufacture.
Industrial labour has begun to shift to the new productive
systems which require a very much smaller number of workers
who must provide greater mental and less manual effort. As
information inputs continue to expand, shop floor workers will
require advanced engineering degrees, just as the American
farmer requires a university degree to take advantage of his
technological back-up.

8 Unemployment

'The liberal reward of labour ... is the natural symptom of increasing national wealth. The scanty maintenance of the labouring poor, on the other hand, is the natural symptom that things are at a stand, and their starving condition that they are going fast backwards.

Adam Smith, p. 176.

HOW BAD WILL UNEMPLOYMENT BECOME?

We are in a transition stage. Just as during the Industrial Revolution there were profound changes in employment patterns, focussed principally on the shift from agriculture to manufacturing, so today is there a shift from manufacturing to the service industries in general and the knowledge industries in particular. During the Industrial Revolution there were other shifts as well – the decline of hand-loom weavers, the rise of new specialties, the emergence of information operatives associated with factories (e.g. payroll clerks) and other aspects of the knowledge industry. So today do we see the shift into the knowledge industries. Many semi-skilled and some skilled information operatives (e.g. filing clerks, typists, bank tellers and estate agents) are being, or will be, displaced. The outlines of the major industry of the twenty-first century (after the information economy), the 'human relations and psychological satisfaction' industry, begin to emerge.

Tens of thousands, sometimes millions, of people suffered severely from the spells of unemployment associated with the evolution of the industrial economy. It is said that those who do not learn from the mistakes of the past are condemned to repeat them. At the beginning of the 1980s it seemed no one had learned very much. To aggravate matters the time span had changed. The full impact of steam power was spread over a century – that of the micro-electronic technology, over no more than two to three decades, probably less. By the early 1980s the better part of a decade has already passed.

Forecasts of UK unemployment in the 1980s vary. R. D. Parslow has listed some of these. They range from a UK government projection of 4 million unemployed by 1990 to 4.7 million unemployed by 1983. It is not the purpose of this book to debate the subject but some comments are in order. Many of the more 'optimistic' forecasts represent a serious effort to obtain specific figures on which to judge the impact of micro-processors. These efforts are commendable and the work needs to be done and expanded. Such research ventures need to be supported over a period of time. In particular, their specific forecasts within each industry, and even within specific companies, need to be monitored over a decade to see how closely the forecasts fit the actual events.

What is often overlooked in the employment forecasts is that almost no employee is directly displaced by new technology. It is almost never a case of old Charley having to leave because a robot is coming in, or Mary being made redundant by a word-processor. Rather it is the move to the Third World (e.g. steel from Europe to Latin America), the 'good times/bad times' paradigm (as we are likely to see in base petrochemicals), or the 'steady displacement' model closing off opportunities for young people (as in printing).

A second misleading factor is a narrow preoccupation with a single technology such as micro-processors. As we discussed earlier in connection with farm productivity or the Port of New York, there are many different kinds of technology involved in the displacement of labour by technology. What makes the micro-processor so important is that it is a meta-technology. But much of its impact will come in conjunction with other technological developments. It is very difficult to assess the additive, and sometimes synergistic, effects of these new technologies; it becomes very easy to ignore them and greatly to underestimate their impact.

Third, many estimates are made by talking to managers and other experts in the field. This method is notoriously unreliable.

Many of these experts are technological illiterates – many managers have no feeling for technology until they are being crippled by it. An excellent example of this (reported by the *Financial Times*, 25 September 1979) is the series of forecasts made by Ericsson's between 1974 and 1978 as to the production and sales of its electro-mechanical telephone exchange equipment which dropped from about 1,200 million Swedish Kronars at its peak in 1975 to about 200 million in 1979. Conversely, the forecasts made for its electronic telephone exchange equipment were equally naive as it rose from about 100 million in 1974 to over 600 million in 1979. The simple insight that electronic devices were going to displace electro-mechanical ones during the late 1970s would have provided a much more reliable forecast. Unfortunately, not only managers, but many engineers,

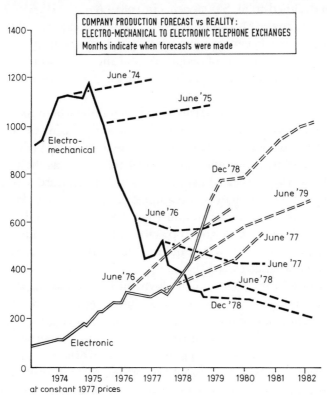

scientists and other technologists, (the products of a narrow education), have no feeling for what is happening outside their own specialty. They are often overtaken by developments in fields related but beyond their intellectual horizons.

Last, it is always safer professionally to be on the conservative side. It is the 'wild' forecasts which lose technocrats their credibility. Perhaps that is why Lord Rutherford in 1933, when asked when we would harness atomic energy, replied 'Never.' Nine years later the first atomic pile went critical.

In the late 1940s the Swiss produced 80 per cent of the world's watches. By the early 1980s that share had been reduced to less than 25 per cent. The Swiss believe that their biggest problem has been the strength of the Swiss franc which rose in value from $US 0.23 in 1971 to as high as $US 0.70 in the mid-late 1970s, then declined to $US 0.58 cents in 1981 (*Business Week*, 5 May 1981, p. 103). This undoubtedly hampered exports. But the changing market must have contributed significantly as well. Hundreds of millions of people around the world were buying micro-electronic watches which were cheaper, more reliable, more accurate and tougher.

Actually, in absolute terms, that is in numbers of units and in value, Swiss exports held remarkably constant during the 1970s. The Swiss were slightly better off in 1980 than 1970 (Federation of Swiss Watch Manufacturers, April 1981). It was their share of the world market which had declined. But in order to stay competitive, they had to streamline their operations. In 1960 there were 2000 companies; in 1970 there were 1000; by 1981 there were less than 500 (op. cit.). In 1970 the number of workers in the Swiss watch industry totalled 89,448; in 1980 it was estimated at 47,200.

In Britain the rise in unemployment is well known. What is often overlooked, and what is even more serious, is the loss of jobs. While unemployment rose by 566,000 during the fifteen-month period between mid 1979 and late 1980, the employment declined by 770,000. This gap in missing workers, which was continuing to widen, is doubly surprising since the population of working age was increasing at a rate of 200,000 per year.

Obviously the job market was shrinking substantially faster than the unemployment rolls were registering.

Only a fool would look into the crystal ball and not tremble.

THE SOCIAL AND POLITICAL CONSEQUENCES OF UNEMPLOYMENT

What would be the social and political consequences of an unrestrained rise in unemployment, in particular of youth unemployment? In 1981 the official overall unemployment rate exceeded 10 per cent, with about 50 per cent unemployment among the youth of ethnic minorities and manual and semi-skilled workers. One of the first social manifestations consisted of a rise in violence and crime. Inner city riots in the UK manifested themselves in the early 1980s as frustrated youths vented their anger against society. The phenomenon parallels similar events in the US in the 1960s. According to another report, violent attacks on the staff of London Transport in 1979 increased by 50 per cent, about three-quarters committed by persons under 21. Vandals caused an estimated £15 million worth of damage to school buildings, over £3 million to British Rail property and £1 million to London Transport. 13,000 assaults on police were reported.

The tendency to commit acts of delinquency and crime is highest amongst those youths with marginal employment records. For vulnerable youths, therefore, a significant reduction in employment opportunities probably tends to shift the balance in favour of crime. Although there are other factors involved in leading young people into a criminal sub-culture, a major contributing cause must be the ease or difficulty with which it is possible to obtain legitimate – and satisfying – employment. Whatever the interaction, in general rising crime rates, particularly crimes against property, do tend to correlate with rising unemployment rates. Returning to Bradford as a case study, an analysis of 124 cases on probation in 1973 for crimes against property showed an unemployment rate of 70.4 per cent as against 2.5 per cent for the general population. In 1976 an analysis of 110 cases on probation for similar crimes showed an unemployment rate of 87 per cent as against a 6.7 per cent rate for the public at large. A substantially smaller sample relating to violent crimes indicated that 50 per cent of the offenders were unemployed in 1973 and 75 per cent in 1976. It is always difficult to interpret statistics of this sort. However, they are clearly consistent with the view that delinquent behaviour is associated with youths who have marginal employment records. It takes no great leap of imagination to wonder whether greatly increasing the number of unemployed youth would not greatly increase the pool of potential criminals. This proposition gains additional credence if one considers that within those socio-economic groups which are substantially disadvantaged in the present economy, there appear subcultures in which criminal behaviour may be viewed as an adaptive reponse to the socio-economic environment. In such an environment criminal acti-vities conducted successfully provide the individual with material, social and psychological rewards.

It is the social and psychological rewards of criminal be-haviour which bear further scrutiny. Human beings have a large number of psychological requirements. One of these is the need for security, another the need to feel useful. A job helps fulfil these needs because the job itself is a contribution to the welfare of the community, and because the earnings from that job help support individuals or their family.

When a job is lost individuals are not only deprived of income but often also of a sense of worth. In addition the loss of a job puts individuals under other psychological stresses. Regular contacts with workmates are lost. There is a loss of social iden-tity. Furthermore the time structure of the working day and week is lost. There is no enforced activity and no motivation to get things done. A gloomy lethargy may set in, which makes simple tasks, such as getting up and dressed, too much of a chore to bother with. There seems to be so little point in doing it. Demoralisation leads to impotence. A self-fulfilling prophecy settles in the mind of the jobless: 'There are no jobs, and even if there were, I wouldn't get them.' Therefore why bother? This pattern becomes reinforced at interviews. Demoralised indivi-duals, convinced that they will be unable to persuade a prospective employer to pick them out from all the others, retreat behind a psychological defence barrier which says: 'I don't care anyway!' What demoralised individuals often convey to the interviewer, therefore, is apathy – with disastrous results. Employers can always risk taking on someone a bit slow, or a bit awkward, providing they are eager to learn. But someone who doesn't care ... that's a dead loss. Therefore the prophesy of an unsuccessful interview has been fulfilled – but who cares anyway?

With luck individuals come out of this vicious cycle of demoralisation spontaneously and get going again. However, such a constructive path almost always involves positive external forces. In their absence, two things happen. Either the demoralisation becomes a permanent personality feature and very often such individuals become involved in escapist behaviour (which may include an increasing reliance on drink or drugs), or individuals rebel and refuse to accept the negative self-image and become antisocial. If there already exists an antisocial subculture then it becomes not only easy and natural, but psychologically necessary, to join that subculture.

With luck an antisocial subculture is only symbolic or only mildly violent, such as punk rockers or Trotskyites. However, there exists a whole range, from the mildly criminal to the extremely violent: football hooligans, street gangs, the National Front, IRA, Bader-Meinhoff, Red Brigade, extreme Fascist groups. These are all examples of antisocial groups the backbone of which consists of frustrated youths whose psychological needs are not met by society.

Social services may provide many material needs. But what of the psychological needs of a community in which 50 per cent of its youth suffer unemployment? This situation prevails in the inner cities of the US. It has started to happen among West Indian teenagers in Bradford and other English cities, and it exists among Catholic teenagers in Northern Ireland. For a youth in Belfast, how better to vent frustration, gain prestige among peers and become a 'real man' than to join the fight against the historic enemy? 180,000 new jobs in

Ulster and IRA recruitment would dry up within eighteen months!

The increasing unemployment in the 1980s will set the stage for increasing crime rates and street and political violence. The response from the bulk of the community will range from cries for law and order to extreme right-wing political activity. Certainly the National Front will continue to grow in Britain. There will emerge a great political polarisation between right- and left-wing groups. Europe at the end of the 1980s could look like Europe did at the end of the 1920s. The political responses will reduce the ability to solve problems peacefully; a nuclear holocaust no longer becomes unthinkable.

INADEQUATE OR COUNTER-PRODUCTIVE ANALYSES AND RESPONSES
To Horace we ascribe the adage: 'To have got rid of folly is the beginning of wisdom.' Let us look at some of the current policies and stratagems designed to improve the employment situation but which are, in fact, inadequate or even counter-productive.

The 'unproductive workers' theory
First there is the 'work harder' response. Workers are overpaid; they have priced themselves out of the market; if they would only work harder and strike less, then productivity would rise; rising productivity would increase the country's international competitiveness which, in turn, would lead to business expansion and more money and jobs for everybody.

This analysis is partly correct. However, a closer analysis of productivity shows that very little has to do with 'working harder'. One is reminded of Charlie Chaplin in his classic film *Modern Times* – arms flailing away in order to keep up with the increasing speed of the assembly line. Significant productivity increases are brought about by improved organisation coupled with advances in technology, utilising increasingly skilled operatives. 'Working harder', by itself, can only result in a marginal increase in productivity. Charlie Chaplin's productivity could have been increased tenfold by providing ten robots to do his job, even if he spent most of his time sitting around drinking coffee or listening to the radio.

British wages are at the bottom of the post-industrial countries (at the top are Belgium, Holland, West Germany and Switzerland, then the US, then Italy, Canada, France and Austria, then Japan, finally the UK). If British workers are underproductive, it reflects incompetent management. This includes management's ability to transcend the traditional polarisation in Britain dating back to the last century. Managers are supposed to manage. Often the greatest impediment to working around those historical traditions is the hide-bound mentality of management itself.

The Luddite response

Second, there is the 'Luddite' response: since the beginning of industrialisation, there has always been a significant sector of the labour community whose response has been to stop the machines, or even to destroy them. The extreme example is that of Anton Möller, a sixteenth-century inventor in Danzig (Gdansk), who devised an automatic ribbon loom in 1586 which allowed an unskilled person to weave merely by pressing a lever. The city council ordered him strangled.

The Luddite response can in no way be considered irrational. It is merely an effort to counter the threat to livelihood or at least the quality of life. It is certainly no more irrational an approach for trade unions than the 'it's the workers' fault' response is for management. Nevertheless, it is also counterproductive. Given the transnational nature of productive enterprises, it is foolish to try to stop the introduction of technology in one country while it emerges in another. Such a policy merely gives the other country competitive advantage. A Luddite response causes the decline and ultimate collapse of those national industries not accepting the new technology.

Even if it were possible on an international level to stop the introduction of such new technology, it would still not be really helpful to global society as a whole. The reason the new technology is successful is because, in fact, it is better. It produces things cheaper, or of higher quality for the same price, so that all the consumers benefit. We have no right to deprive consumers who, after all, include the workers and their families, of improved cheaper products. Much of the rise in standards of living throughout the industrial revolution, and now in the post-industrial society, has reflected the fact that, in terms of real income, virtually every kind of goods is cheaper. One need look only at how people are dressed or how much better they eat, compared with a hundred years ago, to ascertain this fact. Furthermore, it is the business of global society to raise productivity faster than population. If we do not, we will only set the stage ultimately for a nuclear confrontation between the haves and the have-nots. It is imperative that we accept new technology where it improves productivity.

Protectionism

Third, there is the 'protectionist' response. This is not unrelated to the Luddite response. It attempts to prevent the consumer from benefitting in the interest of saving jobs. Like the other approaches, it is partly correct. It is certainly not irrational and it is a view promulgated not only by trade union leaders, and managers of industries threatened by cheaper or better quality imports, but also economists such as those at Cambridge University's Department of Applied Economics.

The trouble with the protectionist response, aside from penalising the consumer and depriving other people (e.g. in Third World countries) of jobs, is that it cannot be a long-term solution. Propping up relatively inefficient operations by import protection will do nothing for exporting those particular goods or services. To make matters worse, sooner or later, import restrictions by one country lead to retaliation by other countries. For example in July 1980 Britain imposed unilateral controls on Indonesian blouses, trousers and woven shirts. A few months later Indonesia introduced a moratorium on new orders involving British firms. British Aerospace lost an aircraft order worth £40 million and the disagreement was beginning to jeopardise export orders worth up to £500 million. By late November the

Davy Corporation appeared to have lost a contract for the design and construction of a £100 million methanol plant. What this means is that import controls in one sector begin to threaten the export of those goods and services in other sectors which are internationally competitive, presumably because they are efficient. This results in a loss of jobs in the efficient enterprises. So the risk with import protection is that, in the long run, the problems of unemployment are merely shifted from the less viable to the more viable industries within a country, or alternatively unemployment is exported to countries whose imports are being kept out.

Protectionism makes sense when one wishes to nurture a young, emerging industry, where one wishes to train a skilled work and managerial labour force. This has been the historical practice of countries for a long time as new industries spread from one country to another and is true today for many countries picking up new industrial technology. For western countries it might make sense to adopt protectionist policies as an alternative to government subsidies for young, emerging high-technology goods and services for a clearly stated, limited number of years. The purpose in these instances, however, is to educate a potential labour force in new ventures, rather than protect jobs in dying industries.

Laissez-faire

Fourth, there is the '*laissez-faire*' response. This is based on the assumption, borne out by history, that in the long run things sort themselves out. We have lived through a long history of technological change. People who were pushed off the farms ended up in manufacturing industries. Hand-loom weavers were displaced but new jobs emerged elsewhere. Think of all the jobs the development of electricity or cars created.

Again, the idea is partially correct, but as Professor Chris Freeman, of the Science Policy Research Unit at Sussex, has pointed out, as far as employment is concerned, technical change is a double-edged sword. It can lead to completely new industries and jobs, but it can also lead to the displacement of labour. The assumption that these processes are automatically in balance simply does not work out in practice. History is filled with examples of large numbers of displaced labourers, from hand-loom weavers in the North of England in the 1830s to textile machine workers in New England in the post-World War II period. The advent of the micro-processor involves a meta-technology which will continue to upset employment patterns in the 1980s greatly.

In the light of historical experience it would be foolish not to consider the examples of the Port of New York, the Nippon Steel Company or Bradford Metropolitan Council as fore-runners of future trends. The question is not so much whether the examples cited will become commonplace throughout the rest of commerce and industry, but at what rate. In view of the fact that micro-processors have become extremely small, cheap and reliable, and there is a growing body of skilled and sophis-ticated labour which knows how to apply these devices, it is not unreasonable to expect a dramatic impact over the next ten to fifteen years. A *laissez-faire* policy may work over the long run, but it is much too risky if it allows millions of unemployed youths to pile up in the meantime.

Monetarism
Fifth, there is the 'monetarist' response. It views unemployment as a manifestation of a flabby, overpriced, non-competitive industry whose energy is further sapped by inflation, high tax-ation and government overspending. The solution is to squeeze out the non-competitive industries, reduce inflation and taxa-tion (in part by reducing government spending) and create a climate of business confidence which allows business expansion. Along with such expansion will come an increase in jobs. One way to achieve this desirable chain of events is to decrease the money supply – thereby increasing the value of the money. In Britain increasing the value of the currency would cause the pound to buy more abroad – thereby making imports cheaper. This will help to reduce rising prices and check inflation. At the same time increasing the interest rates will cause a decline in

borrowing and spending. On the other hand, foreign purchasers would have to pay relatively more for British goods. Inefficient producers in Britain would, therefore, face the twin threat of decreased overseas orders and increased competition at home from cheaper imports. If they could not improve their performance to meet this competition, they would go out of business. The way to reduce prices and combat inflation is first to decrease government spending and second to raise interest rates. Such steps, in their own right, further accelerate the decline of inefficient enterprises. First, the government is a major consumer; by reducing its own rate of consumption it, directly or indirectly, increases competition at home. Second, higher interest rates make it more difficult for companies with cash flow problems to survive adversity.

In principle, this sort of approach is perfectly logical and in practice it is partly correct. The trouble is that although the logic may be impeccable, some of the assumptions are faulty. The major flaw stems from the inability to distinguish between the economy as a total system and the money supply as a subsystem. This failure in conceptualisation leads to two major and, in a sense, opposite problems. On the one hand, the efficiency of the action taken is much less than expected. This is because the monetary system is not a closed national system – it is a very leaky transnational system. It is like driving a piston into a cylinder with a lot of holes in it. The efficiency is much lower than the theory would predict. On the other hand, monetary actions may have a much wider effect than anticipated – they may affect much more than a few marginal enterprises.

The price of goods and services is, in part, a reflection of the cost of production. This cost is a composite of the costs of the various inputs: land, labour, capital, energy, raw materials and components. As the cost of capital goes up, so does the price of the product. Furthermore, although obtaining capital may not be a serious problem for companies which are well-established, particularly multinational companies, it is disastrous for new businesses trying to start. And it is precisely in this area that the new jobs are frequently generated. It is also new ventures which are more likely to become involved with new technology, which increases productivity. Thus, in the short term, by making money more expensive, inflation goes down. But if it cripples new ventures, it cripples future productivity, thereby setting the stage once more for future inefficiencies and future inflationary pressures.

The application of tight monetary doctrines can lead to a serious recession either if the policy is too inflexible or if the system is not monitored properly. The analogy can be made with a space ship. Firing the rockets to accelerate or decelerate does not lead to an immediate response. There is a delay before the full impact of either manoeuvre is stabilised. This tends to lead to 'overshoot': actions designed to alleviate a bad situation frequently do the opposite. They actually aggravate it.

Part of the monetarist tactic is to reduce public spending. However, coupled with higher interest rates and a strong currency, this leads to further unemployment. It is estimated to cost the government around £5000 per year to support a person on welfare (*Financial Times*, 18 August 1980). This includes the money actually provided, the administration of the programme and the revenues lost to the government as a result of unemployment. Another estimate (M. Timbrell in *Lloyds Bank Review*, April 1980) considers the cost to the Exchequer at £4000 per year, with another loss of £3,000 per year to the economy as a result of lost output. At £5,000 per year, two million unemployed in 1980 were costing the government about £10,000 million pounds. Economic policies, dogmatically applied to systems not fully understood, are likely to aggravate problems, not solve them.

Job-creation
Sixth, there is the job-creation approach which has a mix of supporters, including traditional Keynesians, who look to an expansion of public-sector spending to stimulate the economy, and groups primarily concerned with the social and political implications of unemployment. As far as this latter group is con-

cerned, anything which will 'keep the kids off the streets' is all right. They are not particularly concerned about the productivity of job-creation schemes. However, engaging large numbers of people in unproductive work will, sooner or later, lead to serious inflation: useful products and services are not being produced. Those employed in this manner merely become consumers competing with others for existing products. The resulting 'sellers' market' leads to rising prices.

Although digging a nation-length ditch and filling it in again is wholly unproductive, putting people in the army, or putting them to work producing steel which nobody wants, is almost as bad. Unfortunately, a good part of the job-creation programmes of the late 1970s appeared to be involved with jobs which really did not contribute to the country's wealth. Part of the problem reflects the fact that many administrators involved with shaping these programmes lacked the experience, and perhaps the imagination, to generate wealth-creating government-subsidised jobs. Alternatively, they are trapped into thinking about these matters within an industrial (rather than a post-industrial) context. An example of job-creation within an industrial paradigm is illustrated by the De Lorean story in Northern Ireland. The De Lorean factory was to manufacture an advanced American sports car selling for around $US11,000, according to 1977 estimates. The car was to have a number of advanced production and design features, including a revolutionary elastic reservoir moulding process. By 1981 the factory was expected to turn out 20,000 cars per year and employ a workforce of 2,000. The government, in its wholly justified eagerness to create jobs in West Belfast, provided many incentives to get the factory established, not the least of which was the supply of tens of millions of pounds as 'repayable loans'. By the summer of 1980 the original sum of £53 million was supplemented by another £14 million of government funds even though the venture began to look increasingly unreliable. The estimated selling price had shot up from $US11,000 per car to somewhere between $US18,000 and $US20,000, where it would compete with the Chevrolet Corvetter which was selling at

$US14,500. The revolutionary elastic moulding process had
been abandoned. Production was to start in October 1980
employing only 400 with a rise to 800 by the end of the year.
The company could see full employment for 2,000 only if it went
to full production in 1981, turning out 30,000 (instead of 20,000)
cars per year. By 1982 it had gone bankrupt.

The use of £67 million to provide 2,000 jobs amounts to
almost £35,000 capital investment per job in a world economy
which can produce far more cars than can be sold. Contrast
these figures with an expansion of the university system in the
United Kingdom. In Britain, about £800 million was spent on
universities and student grants in 1976-7. This sum provided
education for over 250,000 students and employed an estimated
80,000 people within the system. If one accepts university education as a means of gainfully occupying time (by adding information value to human capital), then the annual cost per person
gainfully occupied is less than £3,000. In a post-industrial
society, where is the money better spent: maintaining the jobs
of machine operatives in over-staffed manufacturing industries,
or developing a new generation of high-level information
operatives?

The major problem confronting western governments in the
1980s is the need to devise ways of effecting a smooth transition
from an industrial to an information economy – to shift labour
from the manufacturing to the knowledge industries. In part
the answer has to involve a massive expansion of an updated
education system to provide new, mainly information skills
which will be useful in a post-industrial economy. However,
much more is involved. What is needed is a new way of looking
at the problem, the development of new economic strategies,
the formulation of new social policies.

9 Inflation

'Pennsylvania was always more moderate in its emissions of paper money than any other of our colonies. Its paper currency accordingly is said never to have sunk below the value of gold and silver which was current in the colony before the first emission of its paper money.'

Adam Smith, Book Two, Chapter II.

As with unemployment, there are several distinct mechanisms which cause a rise in prices. These mechanisms may be quite unrelated. For example, in the 1920s the German government printed money to cover the cost of World War I reparations, creating what has been termed 'hyperinflation'. On pay days workers rushed from the factory gates to the bakery to spend their money before it lost its value further. For the government, the declining value of the money meant a shortfall in their budget estimates. The obvious solution was to print more. The result might best be described as a money plague. It took a whole basket of money to buy a loaf of bread. There was so much money around that it became worthless and people were forced to resort to barter.

In the summer of 1945, following the collapse of the German economy as a result of World War II, money had again become worthless and was replaced by bartering cigarettes, chocolate bars, nylon stockings and other goods. It is the spectre of creating worthless money which haunts the monetarists.

In their fear of government action, or fiscal incompetence leading to inflation, monetarists confuse the type of extreme situations encountered in Germany in the 1920s, or in 1945, with instances of rapidly rising prices such as those encountered during 1974-5 and again around 1980. Although there may have been other contributory factors, the chief cause in 1974, and to a lesser extent in 1980, was the rise in the price of oil. In the 1970–73 period, most countries in the West had an inflation rate in the 3 to 8 per cent range. Between 1972 and 1974 the price of oil quadrupled from around $US2.50 to over $US11 per barrel. By 1974 inflation rates had jumped to 11 per cent for the US, almost 14 per cent for France, 15 per cent for Australia, 16 per cent for the UK, 19 per cent for Italy and a whopping 24 per cent for Japan. Only the strong economies of Germany and Switzerland could absorb the oil price shock.

To understand the significance of the relationship between oil and inflation, we need to return briefly to the theory of limiting factors described in chapter 2. The water-wheels and windmills of the Middle Ages began a process in which sources of energy were harnessed to replace human (and animal) muscle power. Although the technologies were much older, it was not until the Middle Ages that this was to become economically significant. This process became vastly accelerated in the eighteenth century by the introduction of the steam engine. In due course most of the steam engines became replaced by electric motors or by internal combustion or diesel engines. The vast increase in all forms of power machinery fuelled the economies of the world. By the 1960s among the cheapest and most convenient ways to supply the energy for all those machines was by burning oil. There seemed to be so much of it around. However, by the late 1960s the rate at which oil was being burned exceeded the rate at which new oil resources were being discovered. The limits to oil were becoming apparent. It was only a matter of time before the price of oil would be determined by the seller, not by the buyer. That overlap from a 'buyer's market' to a 'seller's market' occurred in the early 1970s. Saudi Arabian light crude oil doubled in price between 1970 and 1973, prior to the 1973 Arab-Israeli war. That conflict provided merely the trigger for further dramatic price increases which were already overdue.

Virtually every material product consumed has, as a part of its price, energy and transportation costs. If it is a loaf of bread, the price will include the energy for driving the farmer's tractor, for milling the wheat and for baking the bread. The price also includes the cost of transporting the wheat, the flour and perhaps the bread itself. The farmer who grew the wheat had to pay energy and transportation costs for his tractor, his fertiliser and his seeds. If the principal source of energy in an economy is based on burning oil, and if oil is the major source of transportation fuels, whether directly as petrol or diesel fuel, or indirectly as electricity for electric motors, then clearly there is virtually no material product which is not going to be affected by the price of oil. Add to this a number of oil-based products such as synthetic fibres and plastics, and it becomes clear why a rise in the price of oil must lead to a rise in the price of all goods. Nor is it surprising that as oil prices stabilised, then declined, the inflation rate should also decline.

The answer to an oil price-induced increase in prices is, as we have already discussed, to find substitutes. Cheap North Sea gas, for example, cushioned some countries against the rising oil prices. This approach, that is, to find substitutes or decrease oil consumption, is in marked contrast to the monetarist approach to the problem. The former combats the effects of rising energy costs by developing new technology; the latter, by manipulating finances. It is probably safe to say that we will never again see the kind of heavy-handed application of monetarist doctrines that we are witnessing in the early 1980s. The motives of the Thatcher administration are commendable; but the theory is wrong. The theory says that inflation is the cause of low economic growth and this is at the root of the unemployment problem. Once inflation has been overcome, growth and employment will follow automatically. To rephrase Emanuel Kant, there is nothing so impractical as a bad theory. Heavy-handed monetarism is not only unable to cope effectively with inflation; it also creates horrendous unemployment problems.

We have already indicated that most of the price rise in the mid-1970s and around 1980 was attributable to rising energy costs as oil began to become a limiting factor. At other times other factors may become limiting, for example, skilled labour. When that happens, wages rise. As with oil, there exists no product which does not have labour costs as part of its price. Again, prices will rise as wages go up. Inflation, in the form of rising prices, is a mechanism which brings consumption into line with resource limitations. It does not matter whether the resource is oil or labour.

The pressure of inflation is felt all over the world. In fact, Third World countries suffer much more. The reason for this global state of affairs is that not only is the world population expanding, but that average living standards continue to rise. That is, not only are there more people, but each person is, on average, consuming more. Where, for example, did the poor Greek peasant go? He now owns a car and a television set. This story is repeated in many other parts of the world. Thus there is a greater global pressure on basic raw materials (such as oil) and even, at times, on manufactured goods. The process has a historical parallel in the marked population increase and ur- banisation of Europe in the sixteenth century. It was accom- panied by a marked rise in prices; the prices of basic foodstuffs rose to four or five times their original level. Just as oil had become a limiting resource in global economic growth in the 1970s, so good cultivable land had become the limiting factor in European economic growth in the sixteenth century. This land shortage, leading to rising food prices which always re- mained ahead of sixteenth-century wages, may well have led to the profound discontent of the Brabant textile workers. These workers joined the rebellion which ultimately freed Holland from Spanish rule. The shortage of land must also have been the primary motive for draining the polders. Thus Holland solved its sixteenth-century economic problems – it got rid of Spanish taxes (a consumption item) and, more importantly, it increased its agricultural productivity. The accumulation of capital was funnelled into a great expansion of all forms of commercial activity, including banking. This led to further capital formation. By the middle of the seventeenth century the Dutch had achieved their 'Golden Age'.

In view of the transnational nature of post-industrial econ- omies, manipulating national monetary systems is hardly likely to work. That is, not only are national monetary measures not able significantly to affect global resource shortages, but national monetary measures can no longer cope effectively with an international monetary system. This showed up clearly in 1981 when the US raised its prime interest rates. The UK and other European governments then had to choose between raising their own interest rates or accepting a devaluation of their currency against the dollar. This latter would, of course, be inflationary.

Furthermore, the equations of Fisher, dear to the hearts of monetarists and orthodox Keynesians alike, assume closed national systems. These no longer exist. Thus the monetarist pre-occupation with the significance of a category of capital called sterling M3 overlooked the amount of sterling purchased by foreign institutions and individuals, and, similarly, the amount of Eurosterling and other forms of overseas capital held by UK residents. Needless to say, the erratic swings and growing tensions in the foreign exchange markets are a source of deepening concern to the leaders of the world's major central banks.

There is only one effective long-term remedy to inflation – identify the limiting factor or factors and devise ways of countering their adverse effect by increasing productivity or finding substitutes. This invariably involves new technological and organisational ways of doing things. Another effective strategy is to expand wealth creation in some other area so that one can afford the increase in price caused by the resource in short supply. This latter process has been taking place throughout history and may be illustrated by pointing to the last few decades; in spite of continuous rising prices, the standard of living has continued to improve. For example, in the two decades between 1956 and 1976 the consumer price index in the UK increased about 3.5 fold. However, during this period the basic weekly wage went up 5 fold, even though the number of hours worked declined by 12 per cent. The pound sterling was worth about ten times more in the early 1930s than in the early 1980s. Yet who would want to go back to the living standards of the 1930s?

It is not the value of money which should concern governments, but the standard of living. The way to a continued improvement in the living standards is to generate the knowledge needed to generate the wealth. A single-minded, almost neurotic, preoccupation with inflation which fails to pay attention to other aspects of the economy – in particular unemployment – is bound to lead to grief.

10 Recommendations: I
New economic strategies

'No large country, it must be observed, ever did or could subsist without some sort of manufactures being carried on in it. . . . In every large country both the clothing and household furniture of the far greater part of the people are the produce of their own industry.'

Adam Smith, Book Three, Chapter III.

So wrote Adam Smith at the beginning of the Industrial Revolution. In the present, early days of post-industrial economy, how great a part of clothing and household furniture need a country produce by its own industry? How much excess need it produce to pay for its imports?

One of the great misperceptions of contemporary economic thinking centres on the hue and cry about 'We must be competitive in world markets'. If we are not, if we do not sell enough abroad, goes the argument, the industry will close down with a concomitant decrease in the balance of payments on the one hand and loss of jobs on the other. This concern is expressed in one form or another by virtually every country with a large manufacturing sector. Britain is no exception. Therefore although we will examine the proposition for Britain, the principles will, with modification, apply to all countries.

As with so many other cherished beliefs, there is enough truth in the matter to make it believable and enough error to mislead. In a frenzy to sell goods abroad or prevent the penetration of a foreign manufacturer into the home market, expensive marketing operations are undertaken in markets already glutted, industries are subsidised, sometimes at great public expense, and there is continuous pressure from manufacturers and trade unions to impose ever higher tariffs and other import duties on foreign competitors entering the UK market. Because so much is at stake, the matter becomes fraught with emotion – rhetoric prevails over reason.

Let us unravel the matter. The loss of an export item does indeed bring about a change in the balance of payments and a loss of jobs. And this is also true when a domestic market is lost to foreign imports. The problems are real, it is the solutions which are specious. For example, the answer to Britain's decline in the steel or automotive industries is not necessarily to pump all sectors of these industries and make them competitive at any cost. The world has steel-producing capacity to excess. Many other countries have cheaper labour, cheaper raw materials, better technology or a combination of these. Therefore the comparative advantage of producing various kinds of steel lies with them. For British steel, only two types of production make sense: specialised products which are better made in Britain, or prestige items, for example 'Sheffield Steel', which still commands respect. In fact, profitability in the late 1970s in the steel industry has generally been at the high-technology end of the product line. A similar case can be made for automobiles where Land-Rovers and Rolls-Royces could continue to command a significant share of the world market. In other cases the answer is to come up with entirely new products like wave-power electricity generators, new kinds of oil prospecting and oil-drilling ships and rigs, devices for extracting thermal energy from tropical oceans and mid-ocean kelp farms, which the world does not yet possess. Britain's greatest export success came during the early phases of the Industrial Revolution when the rest of the world did not yet have machine-woven textiles or steam locomotives. Britain's comparative advantage in manufactured goods became so great that by the late nineteenth century it became a net importer of food.

It is no shame in a post-industrial economy to become a net importer of manufactured goods. It really would not matter in the slightest if Britain produced not a single steel beam, car or ship and imported the whole lot, providing alternative products and services were exported to maintain a reasonable balance of payment and alternative employment was found for the employees of the displaced industries.

There are, in fact, some very good reasons for encouraging the imports of cheap steel, cars and ships. There is the obvious advantage to the consumer (which includes all workers). It also leaves jobs in parts of the world which desperately need jobs. This second point should be considered not only in altruistic terms, but as a positive contribution to global political stability at a time when the nuclear technology is spreading. Third, any process which ties nations irreversibly into a global economic network is a step towards global political integration and peace.

ALTERNATIVE STRATEGIES

What then should be the alternative strategy? A post-industrial country (like Britain) should de-emphasise its share in the world market of traditional industrial products. If it insists on staying in the global manufacturing sector, then it must create unorthodox new products. The paradigm is Japan, which recognises that its share in consumer durables sales will decline. Japan has responded with a conscious national policy of moving upstream technologically and has engaged in massive investments in robotics. The world does not have many robots as yet. But there will clearly emerge a need for highly productive, automated and robotised systems in factory, office, store and home. Certainly if the Japanese have anything to say about it.

However, there is no need to stay in the manufacturing game at all. For the US negative balance of payments in the late 1960s and early 1970s were partly reversed by massive exports of agricultural products. For Britain in the late 1970s it was another primary product: oil. It is one of the ironies of post-industrial economies that agriculture and mining, originally pre-industrial activities, rise once again in importance. And then there is the post-tertiary sector, the invisible earnings in international banking, insurance, shipping, air traffic and tourism. For Britain these have always been significant – often creating the difference between surplus and deficit, and they will become crucial in the future.

Once the implications of a post-industrial information economy have been fully grasped, it becomes much easier to understand the nature of future exports. They will tend to shift from the manufacturing sector of the economy back to the primary sector on the one hand and ahead to the knowledge industry on the other. Britain may once again become a net exporter of food as new technologies and organisational techniques create new food producing systems. Similar knowledge inputs into energy and materials' extraction will cause increasing wealth to be accumulated as has already happened with North Sea oil.

It is in the knowledge industry that Britain has its greatest long-term potential. If during the nineteenth and most of the twentieth, centuries Britain's global economic role was that of industrial machine shop, it must now become its post-industrial technical-managerial consultancy and information provider.

There are several ways in which this is possible or, to be more precise, ways in which this has already been happening. The first involves exporting high-technology units overseas, such as constructing a petrochemical plant, or building and staffing an entire hospital. Another way of earning foreign exchange involves providing organisational information services in the form of international insurance, banking or shipping. A third involves students coming to Britain to study. A related fourth involves tourists coming not merely for fun but to partake of Britain's historical heritage (from Stonehenge through the Industrial Revolution) and to look at other interesting things including its art, architecture, literature, drama, farming practices, television programmes, education system, research and technology. Incidentally, one of the major attractions of London as a tourist centre has been its theatres – the arts have always been a major reason for educational tourism, and as such should be given greater recognition as a significant export item.

IMPLEMENTING ALTERNATIVE STRATEGIES

Bertrand Russell is quoted as saying that 'to conquer fear is the beginning of wisdom'. We should stop being afraid of using the government as an effective economic tool. It is, after all, the most important single, economic institution in a post-industrial economy. Its potential is enormous – certainly enough to smooth the transition from an industrial to a post-industrial economy.

The major problem facing western societies is how to effect a smooth transfer of labour from the manufacturing to the knowledge, and other service, industries: how to phase out manual, factory and low-level information workers, including a good deal of middle management and supervisory personnel: how to redeploy the workforce into the new areas of growth: education, information, telematics, research and development, health care, services, tourism . . .

The most important single step any government can take is to engage in a massive expansion of its education system. A properly devised education system would create a versatile labour force and a new generation of entrepreneurs as well as create a multitude of jobs. The expansion in education should be coupled to a massive expansion of research and development, both to absorb the high-level information operatives and, most important, to invest and create the new industries which will generate the material wealth necessary for sustaining a post-industrial economy. During the transition period, to post-industrial prosperity, the government will need to provide construction projects and to support job-generating private enterprises aimed at employing those manual workers, young people and others, too set in their ways to be enticed back into the education system.

One has to differentiate carefully between the proposals put forth here, and classical Keynesian doctrines. Keynesian doctrines are concerned primarily with consumption, and increasing it through government spending with a view to stimulating economic activity. That is, the government is viewed as a consumer, in fact, a super-consumer.

These proposals view the government as having a role in the economy as an investor, and are designed to provide a significant payback to the government, either directly, as when it

collects revenue from wave-power generated electricity, or indirectly, through increased taxes and revenue collected from
increased economic activity.

One of the great tragedies of our time is that we have not yet
developed the theory to cope with the economic realities. It is
as if we were being racked by outbreaks of typhoid and cholera,
and Louis Pasteur had not yet demonstrated the validity of the
germ theory. Confronted with a late twentieth-century economic plague, our responses are analogues to those of early
nineteenth-century society to its outbreaks of epidemics – attri-
buting them to bad air (miasma theory), or the 'will of God'.
Incidentally, both theories were the basis of actions which sometimes did produce favourable results: the miasma theory was
the basis for introducing the underground, covered sewer system
to London; the religious approach sometimes led to a return to
austere, simple country living, which brought a reduction in
infectious contacts. Similarly, the application of contemporary
theories may also bring about improvements. But a good deal
of it reflects luck, not understanding.

FINANCING AND IMPLEMENTATION

The problem is, how does one convert an economy geared to
producing unwanted goods and services to one which is in tune
with the demands of a post-industrial society? The answer is to
clarify the nature and the needs of this post-industrial society –
to gear up to the information economy. This implies that the
government must engage in a massive long-term investment
scheme. Where is the money to come from? There are at least
three possibilities.

The first happens to apply to Britain, but very few other
countries – a windfall – in Britain's case, North Sea oil revenues.

The second is applicable to most countries – existing revenues
and a restructuring of government spending. Questions should
be raised about where money is best spent – propping up an
ageing manufacturing system or expanding higher education?
Is a nation's security better served by massive defence spending
or structuring a healthy economy? Is money better spent sup-

porting people out of work, increasing prison costs, etc., or
training or retraining young people and then putting them to
work creating an improved transportation network?

The third source may not be needed in Britain, but is certainly
a viable and desirable alternative – borrowing. No good busi-
nessman has any qualms about borrowing money when it becomes necessary to develop a new product, market or organisation, once it becomes clear that there is a fairly certain
payback. The big difference is that governments are super-
businesses which must be prepared to invest in areas (e.g. rural
electrification or computers for young children) where the payback may not materialise for a generation.

The need for financing productive government-spending projects comes easier to some governments than others. A study by
the UK's National Economic Development Council cites over
thirty examples of schemes being pursued by other European
governments which are described as 'adjustment policies'. Such
schemes include ones which affect the flow of capital, labour,
restructuring, trade and, of course, technology.

The French government is heavily committed to pushing
'telematiques', i.e. the mix of computers and telecommunications. In 1979 the French PTT announced an investment program for the 1980s to the tune of £3 billion per year to make
France the leader in telematiques. The plan involves increasing
the number of telephone subscribers to 34 million by 1992 (from
14m) and providing each of them with a free viewdata terminal.
Initially this would be used as a substitute for a printed telephone directory and its costs would, in part, be offset by ob-
viating the need to print directories. Also, such an electronic
directory would allow instant entries and other changes instead
of waiting for a year until the next edition of the printed directory appears. In the long run, however, bringing such a viewdata computer terminal into every home would greatly accelerate the development of viewdata (similar to British Telecom's
Prestel) and other technologies relating to the information
society. Among these is facsimile transmission (mass fax), a form
of electronic mail which will merely be promoted, but will not

be underwritten, by the French PTT. On the other hand, all contracts for the supply of the viewdata terminals will be awarded to French firms and the vast production would, it is hoped, bring the costs down to about £50 per terminal. These would give French producers a considerable advantage in world markets. A pilot experiment is to begin with 250,000 computer terminal telephones installed in Ille-et-Vilaine.

The French are rapidly replacing their old electro-mechanical exchanges with electronic digital equipment, introducing packet switching networks for computer link-ups and experimenting with optical fibre transmission cables – a pilot study in Biarritz is scheduled for 20,000 subscribers in 1982. The French PTT, in cooperation with the military, are planning to launch an all-French satellite – Telecom I – to allow French businesses to beam both telephone conversations and computer data from office to office via rooftop and satellite. As French officials were making and implementing these plans, their counterparts across the English Channel were busy telling the Post Office Telecommunications to watch out how much to spend and not to borrow any money for further technological developments (even though there was no shortage of investors prepared to do so).

In Italy the Instituto Mobiliare Italiano (IMI), a government subsidiary, was set to sponsor research and development for example, by offering easy credit for up to 70 per cent of R & D expenditures over a period of 3–10 years or by offering grants (70 per cent repayable if the scheme was successful). In 1968 about £70 million was made available to encourage new technology and applied research in Italian industry. By 1977 the new Act provided about £1.5 billion of which £200 million were to be devoted specifically to R & D.

Holland began a programme in the late 1970s at a cost of approximately £90 million per year to encourage R & D. This included wage costs, costs incurred in obtaining licences and patents, risk capital for high-technology products, support for small firms and funds for development projects at universities. An additional, smaller 'spearhead fund' had been established earlier in 1977, to stimulate promising new industrial and commercial activity in high-technology, high-risk areas. These have included tool and device engineering, environment, energy and offshore industry.

The Swiss have supported programmes to encourage the rapid diffusion of electronics technology. This is not surprising in view of the threat to their watch industry from the introduction of electronic digital watches. The programme includes training personnel for systems development and process control, R & D for electronic watch components (integrated circuits, quartz systems, digital displays, analogue displays, batteries, etc.), establishing a data-bank centre and support of other related research and development.

The West Germans were devoting substantial resources in the early 1970s for ensuring the rapid take-up by their industries of technological developments pioneered by the Americans and the Japanese, by subsidising product and process innovation, particularly in small and medium-sized businesses. The first data-processing programme to aid the semi-conductor industry began in 1967. West Germany has a Ministry of Technology (BMFT) which supervised this programme in close cooperation with the Ministries of Economics and Education. Other key technologies were also supported, and numerous other schemes to aid R & D and innovation also exist, including direct project support, subsidies, tax relief, providing venture capital, low-interest loans, support for the Confederation of Industrial Research Associations, special information systems, working groups on patent exploitation, information transfer from universities and big science establishments, and others.

Similar stories can be told for many other areas of the European economy. No post-industrial economy is likely to be able to support the massive research and development efforts out of its private sector alone. Free market forces do not necessarily provide the incentives needed for projecting several years to several decades ahead.

WORKFORCE POLICIES

It also becomes necessary to utilise the institution of government effectively in the area of employment adjustment. The training schemes provided by the Swedish government for those threatened with unemployment in ageing industries provide an example of using the government in smoothing the transition to a post-industrial economy. France in 1974 introduced a scheme by which workers made redundant were entitled to 90 per cent of their gross pay for twelve months. The scheme has been extended more recently to permit other options for workers in industry with the government providing about a fourth of the funds, while the remainder comes out of funds provided by a federation of employers. As the Japanese experience has shown, workers who feel secure are more likely to accept change. The greatest impediment to change is fear.

Increasingly European workforce policies are shifting from negative policies of job retention by propping up dying industries to positive policies designed to promote mobility of labour. That is, the newer policies enable workers to move from one industry to another, or from one place to another. About a third of the labour force in Luxembourg is employed in the local steel company, ARBED. Almost a quarter of its workforce was eliminated during the 1974–8 period. Of the remaining 20,000 another 3,500 were expected to go over the next five years. A special 'anti-crisis' division was set up to find new occupations for surplus workers, including the training and retraining of workers. Thanks to redeployment, natural wastage and early retirement, there was no redundancy or short-time working in the industry at any time during the recession of the late 1970s.

Italy pays resettlement grants and defrays travelling and removal expenses for workers and their families moving from one locale to another, while they will help companies by defraying recruiting costs.

West Germany pays allowances to employers in regions hit by unemployment for upgrading the skills of their workers (e.g. up to 90 per cent of wages paid during the period of retraining), job-creation and other schemes. The Germans also instituted a law in 1976 to promote the supply of training places in industry and commerce. The law is aimed at young school-leavers to provide them the opportunity for on-the-job training for full professional qualifications.

In the rest of Europe, as in the UK, there are many schemes to help firms in trouble as a result of oil price rises, collapsing overseas markets or recession. Very often such schemes are motivated by the sincere belief that the firms in question deserve a period of support to tide them over a rough patch. In many other cases it is not economic good sense but the spectre of massive unemployment which causes governments to sink enormous sums of money into a particular firm or industry. When such firms are moribund, spending government funds that way is almost as unproductive as digging that Keynesian ditch.

A NEW DEAL?

A better scheme is to create new projects under a Works Projects Administration (WPA) as in the US the Roosevelt administration did. The WPA provided work for manual labourers (e.g. road building), artists (e.g. murals on public buildings) and others. One of the most successful of Roosevelt's 'New Deal' measures was the Civilian Conservation Corps (CCC). Richard St Barbe Baker, the noted British forester, had just completed a 17,000-mile survey of America's forests. He suggested in 1932 to the then Governor Roosevelt the idea of putting 250,000 unemployed youth to work in forestry. Roosevelt, it is said, shot back: 'Couldn't you make it 300,000?' And so they did. The Corps was divided between the Departments of War, Labor, Agriculture and Interior. Agriculture and Interior chose the projects, Labor selected the enlistees and the Army built and ran the camps. Between April 1933 and June 1939 more than three million men had served in the CCC. In 1939 the CCC came entirely under civilian command and developed its own spruce-green uniform. In 1940 the men (in that year alone) planted almost 300 thousand acres of trees at a thousand trees per acre. They carried out insect pest control on almost a million acres, strung almost six thousand miles of telephone wire, carved eight thousand miles of trunk trails, built half a million check dams, almost a thousand water reservoirs, several thousand cabins, latrines, shelters, museums and look-outs, cleared 2,500 miles of firebreaks, spent many hundreds of hours fighting forest fires, moved six or seven million shrubs and trees in the process of land improvement and conservation, checked erosion and contained floods, restored historic sites and structures, made surveys, developed beaches, built bridges, fountains, fire-places, camp-sites, docks, piers, fences, fish nur-series, stocked the ponds and streams with fish, and performed the thousands of other tasks which restored and extended the land and the forests to the American people. The creation of timber, pulpwood for paper, fertile land and the recreation areas produced untold wealth for the USA.

The Roosevelt approach also led to the Tennessee Valley Authority (TVA) which built the large hydro-electric dams of the Tennessee Valley. A massive programme of dam-building for irrigation, flood control, navigation, erosion control and hydro-electric power was coupled to the Rural Electrification Authority (REA), which made an effort to bring electricity to virtually every farm. These combined to provide the physical infrastructure needed for highly productive agriculture.

To put all this into perspective. Would the rapid increase in agricultural productivity, and the general steaming up of eco-nomic capability during World War II, have been possible if the WPA, CCC, TVA, REA and other similar programmes had not created this enormous economic potential during the late 1930s? Remember, the US was the only country in history able to fight a major war and raise its standard of living at the same time. Could it have manufactured an atomic bomb as quickly had there not been a great excess capacity for hydro-electric power around? It is doubtful.

With the 'New Deal' experience of the 1930s and the 1940s as a background, let us return to the UK in the early 1980s. There is an enormous body of under-skilled labour around which is too old, or too set, to be re-educated and which must be employed manually. To absorb Welsh steelworkers and coal-miners, build the Severn barrage. Even if feasibility studies show that the electricity generated will not quite pay back the government's investment in full, by the time one includes £5000 per person per year employed which would otherwise be charged to the government for keeping someone unemployed, the economics of such a venture will become quite attractive. In addition, previous feasibility studies underestimated payback and the barrage probably could be turned into a sound investment. A similar project at Strangford in Northern Ireland appears to be even more promising. A preliminary feasibility study by research workers from the University of Salford and Queen's University, commissioned by the Northern Ireland Economic Council, concluded that a tidal power station at Strangford could produce about 10 per cent of Northern Ireland's present electricity requirements. The project is potentially a commercial proposition.

Another major project is to build the Channel tunnel. The tolls collected should more than pay for the venture as business and tourism pick up. The country needs to expand transport and housing. The construction industry could absorb a great deal of underskilled labour. In each of these instances, the aim should be to employ older workers. Unemployed youths ought to be funnelled into community service such as a CCC-type of organisation, or into the knowledge industry via the expanded education system. For them, the investment must be in an attractive education system with a good information-operative type job at the end of it.

WORK SHARING

Another major step the government can take to reduce unemployment is to encourage work sharing, in particular by a systematic reduction of the work week. Between the early nineteenth and late twentieth centuries, the work week was effectively cut in half. There is no reason why that might not be done again, but this time in thirty-five years. The formula is simple: A 10 per cent reduction in the work week every five years. Ten per cent reduction is not all that much. Proper management planning would cause productivity to decline only slightly. It would mean four hours out of forty; perhaps two hours off Monday morning and two Friday afternoon. The plan would involve a standard 36-hour week by 1985, $32\frac{1}{2}$ by 1990, 29 by 1995, 26 by the year 2000, $23\frac{1}{2}$ by 2005 and 21 by 2010. Although individual trade unions may negotiate a reduction in work times such an effort is wholly inadequate. Furthermore, unions tend not to push for reduction in work times. Workers, when confronted with a choice of more money or less work time for the same amount of pay, almost invariably opt for the former.

For this reason the government should negotiate on an international basis, the way trade agreements are made. A 10 per cent reduction in work time every five years need not require all the signatories to start at the same level (e.g. US vs. Poland). All that is required is that the 10 per cent every five years rate is agreed on. It also is not necessary to enact it into a law binding on all parts of the private sector. Rather, all that is required is that the signatories promise to introduce the plan into all government offices, apply it to all government employees and expect all government prime contractors to abide by the plan. This would have a sufficient impact on the job market to act as a pace-setter. The UK should begin to negotiate first through its EEC partners, then through the OECD; finally, a third round of agreements should be made through the ILO and the UN. Alternatively, the UK should put pressure on the International Labour Organisation to have such multinational arrangements codified.

Although a 10 per cent reduction in work time may not appear to be much, it does represent, in theory, almost a 2 per cent increase in labour requirements every year. In practice this would work out to be much less. It would not, however, be insignificant.

LONDON: OFFICE CAPITAL OF THE WORLD
As the UK unemployment figures rose during the 1970s there remained one bright spot: London and the surrounding part of

the country. As far as unemployment was concerned, this area remained relatively untouched. The basic reason undoubtedly related to the strength of the knowledge industry in the area. The higher quality knowledge inputs into the manufacturing sector were reflected by the relatively higher *per capita* productivity of the workers in this region. As is usually the case, higher productivity and lower unemployment went hand in hand. Both tend to be associated with advanced technology.

For London there was another reason for the low unemployment: structural (technology-based) unemployment had not yet hit the offices seriously during the 1970s. And London was the office capital of the country – no British company of any size could afford not to have an office in London (usually its head office). Lots of offices meant lots of jobs. Lots of jobs means labour is relatively scarce. A scarcity of labour tends to drive up wages. A scarcity of labour coupled with increased labour costs favour the introduction of labour-saving devices which increase productivity. Hence a healthy employment situation tends to be characterised by low unemployment, high wages, high productivity and advancing technology. The huge number of offices and related services in London set the stage for the prosperity for the UK's south-east when compared with the north of England, Wales, Scotland and, of course, Northern Ireland.

The principle of London as the office centre of the UK should be deliberately expanded to cover the international office market. That is, London, should not only be the national centre, but the world centre – a function which it has already achieved to some extent. London has a long and respected history as an international centre for banking, finance, insurance and shipping. Its telephone and telex linkages to other parts of the world are among the best. London is an important centre for the global air transport network. Its office-related labour force, ranging from stenographers to management consultants, is good. Finally, one of its greatest assets is its native language – English.

How to make London pre-eminent as the world's office centre? Begin with an expansion of its communication and transport capabilities. Improve the Post Office system, particularly British Telecom. Get more money and new blood into the system. Develop as rapidly as possible electronic capabilities to create what Joseph Ferreira, vice-president of Diebold, refers to as the 'infinite desk'. To achieve this, existing British Telecom programmes need to be expanded and accelerated. These programmes include installation of System X and advanced teletext systems, gateway systems (e.g. 'Albert') to interconnect various types of electronic information devices such as file stores, printers, visual display units, word-processors, 'smart' telephones, Prestel and the development of a global satellite system. Copper cables should be replaced with optical fibre systems.

There are other systems which need to be explored: videophones for face-to-face tele-conferences, ultimately coupled to holographic systems, potentially useful not only for tele-conferences but also for information storage and retrieval systems (holographic videofiches). There is a need to expand Prestel rapidly, not only in terms of cheaper and better hardware, but also the quality and quantity of information stored. The rapid expansion of Teletel, the French counterpart of Prestel, should be considered as a model.

To make London the office capital of the world, it must be able to plug into systems like Teletel and be able to receive, organise and transmit incredible amounts of information including three-dimensional moving pictures. The communications system must become so cost-effective that offices and companies in other parts of the world will find it cheaper to establish an office in London through which they funnel all their other global contacts rather than establish a separate network of their own.

Similarly, the transportation network must be significantly upgraded. This applies particularly to air travel. As many travellers who have stood around for forty-five minutes waiting for their luggage to reappear can attest: there must be a better way. Smart travellers, of course, take only carry-on luggage – but it should not have to be that way. Better systems must be derived so that the time spent at airports, either outward- or inward-bound, is cut to fifteen minutes, including going through immigration and customs. For luggage, a miniature container-isation system with better designed loading facilities at both the aircraft and the airport might help. This sort of system is more likely to be developed at the individual airline, rather than at the airport, level. Let the British air carriers take the lead by introducing automated check-in facilities and multi-port entry into the aircraft. New systems need to be devised so that any flight can handle fifty passengers per minute in order that 500 passengers may board in ten.

A second area for improvement is the time it takes to get into London from the airports. Clean, comfortable, high-speed, non-stop rail coaches from Gatwick to Victoria running every ten or fifteen minutes during peak periods, and scheduled to coincide with air traffic at other times, would help. The rail coaches should be staffed by customs and immigration officers which process passengers on the way to and from the airport. Cheap helicopter services to transportation hubs such as Pad-dington, King's Cross and Victoria should be explored. What-ever turns out to be London's third airport, a major effort must be made to get passengers into the centre of London in about fifteen to twenty minutes.

In addition to air travel, building a multi-purpose Channel tunnel will not only provide motor and rail link to the continent but help reduce British parochialism. There is still a significant part of British opinion which views itself apart from Europe and in fact fears it. One has the impression that part of the opposition to the Channel tunnel stems from an image of hordes of Napo-leonic troops pouring out of it trampling the British countryside. High-speed, direct rail services between London and Brussels, the EEC capital, will become increasingly important as the European economy continues to integrate. Comfortable over-night sleepers to more distant European capitals, particularly in the east, may also become viable. There should also be an increase in business-related tourism where one member of the family travelling on business brings the entire family.

London hotels leave much to be desired. By most standards they are expensive and their plumbing is relatively poor. These are short-comings which are not universal; they represent an asset which can easily be upgraded. Rooms should have available not only the standard telephone and TV, but Prestel, computer and advanced electronic communication devices. Hotels near airports and railway terminals need to supply an ever-increasing number of conference rooms of all sizes, equipped with the latest audio-visual, computer and electronic communications devices.

In addition to an improved physical communication/transportation/information infrastructure, London must develop an increasingly sophisticated intellectual infrastructure. Not only must the equipment be advanced, so should the people – ranging from the clerical to the consultancy level. Office workers need to know how to operate word-processors, computers and other advanced office machines. Everybody ought to be able to converse in at least two or three languages, and a host of experts should be available in banking, investment, finance, insurance, office organisation, management, industrial relations, public relations, social relations, marketing, advertising, national and international law, editing, accounting, computing, forecasting, technology ... – experts who understand their subjects in a foreign context as well as a British one. This becomes easier as more information becomes available through international data banks (accessed via Prestel-type systems), and with improved communications, the development of multinational consultancy firms. And only a high-level education system can provide the high-level information operatives required to make London the nerve-centre of the business world. An upgrading of the education system should include an expansion of management education and an improvement in the professionalisation of managers. All managers need to be exposed to the concepts of science and technology, and to their history and impact on society. All managers ought to have command of two or three languages.

The expansion of management training programmes should also accommodate large numbers of foreign nationals. The inclusion of foreign students has a number of positive effects well worth any marginal costs incurred by not charging them the full cost of running the institution. It brings in foreign exchange, not only in the form of fees, but living expenses while studying in Britain. People who come to Britain to study tend to become familiar with British goods and services and they are more likely to order British in their future jobs. Further, one of the major benefits of university education relates to the mixing of people. Students learn from each other. The mixing of students of different nationalities helps to break down parochialism and nationalism. Such student contacts will often lay the foundation for future business contacts which is precisely what is needed for making London the business capital of the world. Organising vigorous alumni societies for the various university graduates along the lines of American universities could help maintain such linkages effectively and develop a global network of managers. Such a network will tend to foster economic prosperity and political stability.

Lastly, one should also take into account the extracurricular activities which would induce businessmen to want to come to London. First of all, London is an extremely cosmopolitan city with a substantial historical heritage. Both these features are advertised and promulgated by BBC World Service. The simple act of having the bells of Big Ben resound over the world's airwaves makes one want to listen to them in person. One gains the impression that London is an important place. It becomes a status symbol to have gone there. It must become an even more important status symbol to have conducted business there.

Once in London there is the pleasure of quality television, galleries, museums, guided tours and theatres – in particular the theatres – concerts, opera and ballet, sports events, films, restaurants and night clubs. English pubs, of course, are in a class by themselves. One must not forget the potential for loneliness and boredom of the executive stranded for several nights in a hotel. This also means that the amorous activities of Soho or Shepherd's Market should be expanded, not restricted. The primary concern in these matters should be with public health, not with public morals. The former is real, the latter arbitrary. To make a city into a global business capital it is important to ensure not only that business can be conducted in such a city with ease, confidence and profit, but that it becomes a pleasure to do business there as well. This is why it becomes important to expand funding to the Arts Council and imbue London and the rest of the country with a vigorous cultural life.

England has one other great post-industrial asset. It is a country where people speak English. This is important because English has become the *de facto* global language. It is the language of the sea and airways. It is the language of commerce. It is a compromise language for a sub-continent such as India. It dominates the world airwaves thanks to the Beatles and the BBC, and with American help it dominates television, pop music and the global youth culture. Hundreds of millions of people want to learn how to speak English – let them come to England to learn it. This means expanding BBC overseas services and education facilities at home. Both provide jobs and the latter, aimed at foreign students, earns foreign exchange and provides other benefits.

Strengthening the trend which makes English the global language favours making London the business capital of the world. New York is likely to be its chief rival, although it could be Singapore or Hong Kong. London has an advantage in its historical heritage, and is more cosmopolitan in some ways than New York. It all depends on who does what and when. For example, if one wishes foreign executives to settle in London, the city will need to provide special subsidies for housing and provide special considerations for the education of their children.

It may be necessary to provide other incentives as well, but these two are basic. Every business executive lured to London is a bonus for the city's information economy. If Britain does it right, there should exist no company of any consequence anywhere in the world which can afford not to have a major branch office in London, perhaps even its headquarters.

TOURISM
Making London the office headquarters of the world would provide jobs and foreign exchange for the home counties and

surrounding countryside. How about the rest of the country? One answer is tourism. Tourism can be erratic but it is a large employer of the unskilled and semi-skilled (such as porters, waiters, taxi-drivers and small retailers) and it is an ideal buffer against the vagaries of the international economic climate. When Britain seemed in dire economic straits during the mid-1970s tourists flocked here by the millions. The low value of the pound caused hundreds of thousands to descend from Europe for weekend shopping sprees. As the economic fortunes reversed, so did the tourist flow. By the end of the 1970s more Britons flew to the United States than Americans to Britain.

As with manufactured goods, a successful product fills a need not provided by others. It has to be unique. Britain is hardly the best place for lolling about on sunny beaches. Nor is some of its natural beauty, such as the Lake District, unique. After all, the Alps, the Rocky Mountains and the Himalayas are becoming increasingly accessible to tourists. But the brooding moors of North Yorkshire have a quality of their own. Part of that quality reflects the historical heritage created by books and films – Haworth, home of the Brontës, has become a major tourist attraction.

It is that historical heritage which is a major tourist asset. Stonehenge and other stone circles, Roman fortifications, Gothic cathedrals, and the pomp and colour of the Changing of the Guard at Buckingham Palace, all attract visitors but they are rivalled by other countries such as Greece and Italy. What Britain has, however, is the Industrial Revolution with its canals and railways, its satanic mills and back-to-back houses. As we move deeper into the post-industrial era, the early industrial period will become more and more interesting to us. It is criminal how much of it is being knocked down.

On the other hand, there are interesting instances of preservation and refurbishing. Among the most extensive and interesting of these is the Iron Bridge complex at Coalbrookdale. A different type of effort is illustrated by William Ackroyd and Co., Spinners of Otley, who converted a number of their disused nineteenth-century stone buildings adjacent to their operating mill, into craft workshops. These workshops have been rented to hand-loom weavers, glass blowers, instrument makers and potters. The plans are to open up a waterfront restaurant in the downstairs portion of one of the buildings located on the banks of the Wharfe river, while the upstairs will contain some of the disused and refurbished derelict machinery to form a small industrial museum. Thus a successful manufacturer is diversifying into the leisure industry, converting liabilities into assets.

Not only a cluster of derelict buildings but a whole town can be rejuvenated. Hebden Bridge in West Yorkshire's Calderdale is an example. Following World War II, as the mills closed down and employment opportunities continued to shrink, Hebden Bridge began its steady decline until by the late 1960s it was beginning to look like a ghost town. Then some local people decided to turn things around. Hebden Bridge, nestled in the Pennines, is a beautiful Victorian mill town, surrounded by moors and plenty of history. By making restorations and repairs, the town attracted tourists which provided money for more restoration and repairs. Interesting shops sprang up in the village to cater to the tourists. It also became a nice place to live. At least one group of entrepreneurs settled who, in due course, developed a small factory. As the town recovered its morale, more and more people volunteered to help with the restoration. Hebden Bridge began to acquire prestige. People with money started moving in. So did writers, computer programmers and commuters from Manchester. Whereas much of Calderdale was continuing to decline, things were obviously improving in Hebden Bridge.

Educational tourism will become an important industry in post-industrial economies, as will the leisure industry as a whole. By the late 1970s, tourism had become a bigger industry in Britain than automobiles. The North of England is ripe for educational tourism, centred on the history of industrialism. Show people the restored eighteenth-century lead mines near Grassington. Tell them how the miners used to die, their bodies wasted by lead poisoning in their late twenties and early thirties.

Walk up through the long, dark, underground chimneys and tell them about the young boys working on the inside, scraping off the condensed lead, sometimes suffocating in the fumes as a careless or drunk miner lit the furnace without checking the chimney. Show some of the dark mills in which young children, terrorised and brutalised, toiled twelve hours and more six days a week and on the seventh were beaten in the name of God for falling asleep during lengthy sermons. Those who attempted to run away were literally chained to the machinery. Take people to Bradford, where life expectancy at birth in the early nineteenth century was 18.6 years, and where, early in the twentieth century, one could still find twelve-year-old boys bald at the top of their heads because they worked in the local coal mines where shallow tunnels did not allow the boys to stand up; the only way they could push a cart with a hundredweight of coal up the slope was by crawling on their hands and knees, pushing with their head. Their fathers would have to crawl in those same tunnels for half a mile before they could start earning their daily bread. Show people who enjoy the warmth and the light, the good food and the good health of post-industrialised society the debt we owe our forebears.

Educational tourism centred on the Industrial Revolution should not consist only of showing this or that mill or mine, with a few horror stories thrown in, but begin to organise systematic trips and courses of lectures aimed mainly at school-teachers around the world but which, when properly organised to mix education with entertainment would attract academics, businessmen, professionals and their families.

Field trips should include journeys on trains through beautiful countryside (Manchester to Bradford, or Bradford to Carlisle), coupled with walking tours (such as at Hebden Bridge), coach trips to points of interest and beauty spots such as the Yorkshire Dales, the Peak District and the Lake District, trips on old railways (like the Worth Valley Railway), canals (the Leeds-Liverpool canal), museums such as Bradford's Industrial Museum, York's Railway Museum and, of course, visits to the mills, mines, canals, railway bridges, farmsteads, crofts, back-to-back houses and warehouse districts. And don't forget the many beautiful pubs!

Most of the tourist industry should be in the private sector. However, government, both locally and nationally, must provide investment and leadership to initiate the industry. Once established, the government must continue to coordinate and regulate. Foreign visitors are always easy prey to unscrupulous operators. There is nothing like a reputation for being 'ripped off' for keeping tourists away. If the government does not enforce stringent quality standards, the business will simply melt away without anyone quite knowing why.

To create a viable tourist industry in the North of England requires that the government should expand its present efforts to determine what facilities, programmes and other assets exist now for catering both for the personal and for the educational needs of tourists, and consider how best to upgrade them. The government should support educational ventures in both public and private sectors aimed at attracting overseas visitors. It needs to establish the bureaucratic machinery for quality control, set standards of safety, health, catering and education, provide guidelines for reasonable pricing and develop machinery for prosecuting 'gaugers', or those who fail to maintain prescribed standards. Lastly, it must engage in a massive overseas marketing operation, using both government tourist boards and other agencies, and cooperating with private ventures.

CHEESE AND BISCUITS

> Bordeaux is ... the entrepôt of the wines which grow upon the banks of the Garonne, and of the rivers which run into it, one of the richest wine countries in the world, and which seems to produce the wines fittest for exportation; or best suited to the taste of foreign nations. (Adam Smith, pp 435–6.)

Some countries are known for their fine wines, others for their beers, a third country for its olives and a fourth for its cheese, a fifth for its coffee... The British produce some of the finest cheeses in the world: Wensleydale, Cheddar, Red Leicester,

Blue Stilton, to name but a few. The trouble is the world does not know about them. The same can be said for the light, dry biscuits to go with the cheeses. The matter is largely one of marketing – attractive packaging, attractively priced, properly advertised. Cheese products could be a major export item, especially when single-cell protein for feeding dairy herds becomes a viable technology. Food producing and processing industries should be private but the government must provide leadership and help with the initial marketing campaign, as well as with the research leading to increased production, productivity and quality. It will be the quality of information, that is, the sophistication of the research and development, the new product development, the new marketing strategies, the organisational ability, which will determine the success or failure of these ventures. Expertise as usual, will be the limiting factor, rather than the availability of land, labour or capital.

Cheese and biscuits do not exhaust the list of food and drink exports. Fish and chips, of the northern variety, could travel as well as whisky, chocolates, biscuits, sauces and other quality items which Britain sells abroad. Processed foods for export may not seem as glamorous as steam locomotives, but the world has changed and so have its needs; and Britain, fortunately, has come a long way from its seventeenth-century culinary backwardness attested to by Caracciola when he noted: 'There are in England sixty different religious sects and only one sauce.'

11 Recommendations: II Education

'The expense of the institutions for education ... is ... no
doubt, beneficial to the whole society, and may, therefore,
without injustice, be defrayed by the general contribution of
the whole society. This expense, however, might perhaps with
equal propriety, and even with some advantage, be defrayed
altogether by those who receive the immediate benefit of such
education and instruction, or by the voluntary contributions
of those who think they have occasion for either the one or
the other.'

Adam Smith, Book Five, Chapter I.

In the late eighteenth century it had not yet become necessary
for farmers or workers to know how to read and write. That
need did not become obvious until the Industrial Revolution
was well on its way. Universal public education came to Britain
about a century after *The Wealth of Nations* was written. Victorian reformers only vaguely understood the importance of information in creating and running an industrial economy. Had
they been told that a century later attending school full-time
would be compulsory until age sixteen, they would have been
appalled. To them, it would have been a luxury society could ill
afford. It is not surprising, therefore, that Adam Smith should
have equivocated on the question of whether the expense of
education should be borne by public or private funds.

Two centuries after *The Wealth of Nations* we have moved into
the information economy. A massive expansion of the education
system must be the cornerstone of any government policy designed to ease the transition from an industrial to a post-industrial economy, in order to provide the skilled workforce required
by an information economy. An educated work force tends to
exploit new technology whereas an ignorant one tends to be
victimised by it. This is particularly true for managers. In

addition, a massive expansion of education represents a massive attack on unemployment. The education system is an excellent employer in its own right, ranging from porters and tea ladies to history dons and computer professors. In addition, an attractive education system, perceived to be useful by its practitioners and recipients alike, would keep millions of young people in education and off the labour market. If one assumes a fifty-year working life, each additional year spent in the education system means that 2 per cent of the labour force is tied up.

ELECTRONIC EDUCATION

The use of radio and television for information communication, and the use of computers for information processing, storage and retrieval, represent new technological developments of greater significance than the invention of the printing press. Education television at the pre-school and primary schools levels has come far in the last two decades. In the USA the Children's Television Workshop's 'Sesame Street' and 'The Electric Company' have built up an impressive record of research and practical experience. In Britain the experience has moved well beyond the experimental to the routine, not only with BBC programmes, but also with independent broadcasting, such as Thames Television's 'Finding Out' series. The increasing sophistication of TV aimed at children reflects the increasing sophistication of TV adult 'entertainment' including such programmes as 'Panorama', 'Horizon' and 'The World About Us', whose educational value cannot be overestimated. Nor should educators underestimate the value of historical drama, travel, special series on science or literature and other documentaries. The experience and utility of formal courses involving television, such as those put on by the Open University, will be greatly expanded as cable television becomes available, allowing for simultaneous broadcasts via telephone or other cable links, and as home-video recording equipment becomes less expensive. Combined with other systems, e.g. the Post Office's Prestel, BBC's Ceefax and ITV's Oracle, that colourful box in our living-room will become an information screen displacing tele-

phone directories, travel agents, estate agents, encyclopedias
and even our daily newspaper.

The use of computer-assisted learning is also developing rapidly. It is most easily adapted to, and most needed in, teaching
mathematical skills at all levels. An example of the extensive use
of computer-assisted mathematics instruction is found in the
system developed in northern Ontario. The project began in
the late 1960s under the sponsorship of the Ontario Institute for
Studies in Education and a number of community colleges,
particularly Seneca College in Toronto. Tens of thousands of
students have gone through this programme since then. Students completed the course in roughly one-third of the time
required to do a standard course, with teacher intervention
involving less than 10 per cent of the time, and the cost per
student was reduced to approximately one-third. Most students
liked it: student drop-outs in remedial maths were reduced by
80 per cent, and one girl commented, 'It's the first maths teacher
that never yelled at me.'

A computer can give individual attention which the average
teacher in the classroom cannot hope to give. Properly pro-
grammed computers exhibit infinite patience, never put down
a student and rely on positive reinforcement. They can monitor
a student's progress more accurately than any other means so
far devised, and are getting cheaper all the time. The main
resistance will come from the educators themselves who do not
understand the new technology and are frightened by it. Such
educators, in their ignorance, disparage TV and the computer,
and create a generation gap between themselves and the electronic teaching professionals on the one hand and their students
on the other.

HOME-BASED EDUCATION FOR THE YOUNG

The major shift in technology, then, involves the emergence
of the electronic home-based education capability using the
television screen and the computer terminal as its base, tied via
telephone, airwaves, or local cable television to the local education authorities, a second tie-in to national and international

computer network systems and finally a tie-in to the global library archives. As these networks expand, the home centre will have information available which vastly exceeds the largest city library and which makes owning a mere encyclopedia seem as primitive as owning a Victorian slate to scratch on. Thus, traditional subjects can all be learned at home. Children will learn either by playing 'games' with a home computer, by playing 'games' with friends (using a computer), or by looking at live programmes, films or video-tapes. Coupling computer-based learning with educational TV in the home means that tailor-made, individually orientated education will be able to replace the much less adaptable mass classroom-based education currently imposed on children in western countries.

Finally, we must add to the home-based education system one other ingredient. It is not enough to provide highly sophisticated and advanced electronic teaching devices. There must be a human touch. That touch should be provided by the western world's most under-used resource: its mature citizens. There is reason to believe that the human species evolved post-reproductive females (an anomaly, according to classical evolutionary theory) to facilitate the transfer of information across the generations. That is to say, grandmothers were humanity's first information storage and retrieval system. (This is not to exclude grandfathers, although in the old days they were probably killed hunting wildebeests.) Using older people to provide the cultural heritage and the personal touch would be of enormous benefit to both the young and the old. Each 'grandparent' could meet a group of two or three children for ten to fifteen hours a week, and such a relationship could last for a period of perhaps more than ten years. Parents moving from one locality to another might consider leaving their children in the care of the surrogate grandparent in order not to interrupt their education. This may become perfectly feasible as travel becomes increasingly efficient and cheap.

The upshot of evolving such a system is that young children as they begin to learn to speak become progressively immersed in an information environment which is enormously rich and pleasurable. They will learn most traditional skills on their own or within small groups of neighbourhood children. The efficiency, flexibility and depth of learning will be considerable. By the turn of the century, the average 10-year-old will have mastered the rudiments of calculus, Boolean algebra and other advanced forms of mathematics.

SCHOOL-BASED EDUCATION

During the first decade of a child's life, most of its learning will involve education in its own or a neighbour's home. However, children need to play with other children to facilitate their own emotional growth and to acquire social skills. Such play may take place in 'nurseries', as is the practice today, or it may involve play centres in a neighbour's home (rented by the government). Periods of play alternating with home-based learning also provide rest periods for the grandparent.

As the children grow older, groups of friends will go to school to avail themselves of facilities to engage in sports, laboratory exercises, dramatics, etc., while at the same time beginning to interact with large peer groups. However, school experiences should not be structured strictly in terms of age groups, except where this is appropriate (e.g. certain kinds of team sports). Learning how to handle laboratory equipment, learning how to swim or how to play chess, may best be handled by mixing ages.

One of the primary functions of the traditional school is that of an institutional device for educating for community interaction. School is also a place (and stage) where children are first encouraged to develop organizational skills and to prepare them to assimilate a more systematic body of information. That is, the schools can consolidate a child's information base in a more formal, uniform way – at least where it is necessary to have such uniformity – although in general, the new objective of education will not be to educate for uniformity, but rather for versatility and diversity.

COMMUNITY SERVICE FOR TEENAGERS

As the children approach their teens, a profound shift in interests occurs. Partly as a consequence of changing hormonal patterns, the interests begin to shift to members of the opposite sex and to an enlarging awareness of the community in which they live. Some of the emerging interests reflect a desire to enter the adult world and share some of its responsibility and be accorded some of its status. In the western world university education is sometimes interspersed with work experiences. There is no reason why that principle should not be enlarged at the university level and brought down to the teenage period. Teenagers are not only eager to accept certain job responsibilities, but very much look forward to the financial rewards which give them a measure of independence. In a way, teenagers constitute an ideal underclass: all the mucky jobs in our society tend to be done now by ethnic minorities who stand very little chance of moving beyond those jobs. It usually takes them several generations to move up. In the process, they are subjected to serious deprivation (often denigration) in holding down those jobs.

Consider, on the other hand, having teenagers do all the nasty jobs which society still needs. It is understood that this is part of their service to humanity and it is understood that as they grow up, they move into the better jobs. The use of a teenage labour force should also be coupled, perhaps somewhat later, with a period of 'community service' – a form of national service which is not military, although it may be appropriate to exercise a fair amount of discipline. Certain units, for example, might be used for land reclamation, community work and work overseas. Some youngsters might stay on for further training for a career in the police, fire, ambulance corps or coastguard, which will continue to be an important career sector. Others may become involved in digging irrigation ditches in the Sahel, or planting trees in the denuded tundras in order to improve global productivity. The emphasis should be on global, rather than national, service. In other instances, the work would be done in the local community. The main objectives of such a programme would be to break the school routine and to mature the students by introducing attitudes of discipline, group integration and community service. Provision should be made for students who for reasons of conscience or talent would be excused from such service. In general, however, young people are ideally suited for involvement in service activity which would become their cultural passport to adulthood.

COMMUNITY-BASED EDUCATION
Following the teenage schooling and the community service phase, students would advance into higher education. They might do so only after a period of several years of paid employment or after a substantial period of leisure. Higher education will be a mix of traditional university, coupled with electronic data media, based at home or in a similar environment. Much of the university education of the future will involve students moving around from one institution to another. This trend is developing in the USA, where the credit system allows students to spend one or two years at one institution then shift to finish off at another institution, perhaps even to go through three or four. This makes for a much better education because, first, moving among communities is in itself an education and, second, different institutions have different strengths and weaknesses which can be exploited by a mobile student force. Increasingly, as higher education becomes mixed with appropriate work experiences and with practical applications outside the university classroom, the majority of the population will attain by their mid-thirties perhaps twenty years of schooling. A very substantial minority will have gone on to the equivalent of doctorate degrees.

RE-EDUCATION
Re-educating adults is particularly crucial in the 1980s as large numbers of workers in different occupations are displaced by technology. The emphasis must be on education rather than training for two reasons. Training creates specialists who may glut the market, either because there has been a misperception of the numbers needed, or because a new technology emerges to

displace specialists. Education, on the other hand, creates versatile generalists who can be trained very quickly to fill specific employment niches. The second reason for emphasising education rather than merely training has been stated clearly by Sir Roy Shaw, Secretary-General of the Arts Council. Education and the arts are '... a valuable countervailing influence to the misery and despair that often afflict the unemployed'. Sir Roy urges that we plan for maximum use of adult education and the arts, 'if we want to move towards a more civilised and humane society instead of towards a nightmare of massive enforced idleness, with accompanying angry despair'.

In many instances re-education consists of training in leisure activities such as crafts. From an economic point of view this sounds like a pure frill. However, this type of education, too, can produce substantial economic benefits. Many a person has been alienated from education. Anything that can be done to seduce them back into it and build up their confidence in their own abilities is a positive accomplishment. Furthermore, hobbies can frequently be turned into small businesses. The leisure industry is likely to be a growth area, particularly tourism. Tourists need photographers, caterers, local handicrafts, tour guides and so forth. What is particularly important is that in this type, and all other forms, of education a serious effort is made to encourage the development of entrepreneurial skills. Teach people how to get things organised!

Re-education is already a well-established part of our culture as witnessed by the marked rise in adult and further education. In many instances it is spearheaded by middle-class housewives who have time on their hands or who, for reasons of finance, social background or some other lack of opportunity were unable to move into higher education earlier in life. Many universities in North America and an increasing number in the UK are starting to cater for mature, part-time and extramural students. An increasing number of commercial and industrial companies are also sending their employees and managers on courses or are organising series of in-house seminars.

Among the most exciting of experiments in western education

is the UK's Open University. The use of electronic facilities in the student's own home represents one of the major patterns for future community-based education. One should not, however, overlook one of the most popular aspects of the Open University courses, which is the gathering of students at some particular place during the summer.

A different paradigm in community education is offered by the New School for Social Research in New York City, where the vast bulk of its student body are adults taking evening courses. The importance of the New School is not only that it acts as an intellectual centre, but it also acts as a centre for meeting people.

Lastly, with the continued expansion of global transportation systems, organised travel will become as much a part of education as will the traditional classroom. Moving groups of people to different sites to satisfy different kinds of interest will be a major new industry coupling education with tourism. Museums, education centres, arts festivals and other educational and cultural events will become increasingly an economic asset.

EDUCATION FOR ALL?

Is education possible for everyone? This question resembles the question asked by our Victorian forefathers as to whether it was possible to teach working-class children how to read and write. The problem in many countries today is exemplified in Britain by working-class attitudes towards education. Working-class parents tend to be reasonably positive and helpful about their children's educational prospects in primary school. The primary school tends to concentrate more on the child than on the curriculum. Substantial progress in school reinforces both child and parents' attitude towards education.

Then comes the shift to the secondary system. The older child is now forced to adapt to a prescribed curriculum, dominated by the universities, a system aimed at the culturally advantaged top 20 or 25 per cent of the children. As puberty progresses, youngsters care most about their status with their peers, exploring sexual relations and the world around them. The current

curriculum appears to be of very little relevance. Stresses between teenagers and parents complicate educational motiva-
tions. Communication blocks with adults lead to a 'generation
gap'. Furthermore, in working-class homes, the teenagers are
reaching an age where they might contribute financially to the
parents' household. For the youngsters a job means greater
independence and status within the family. For the family it is
a welcome financial supplement. The parents' attitude is often
that since the children are doing poorly at school anyway, just
as they did, they might as well stop wasting time and get a job.
School becomes increasingly irrelevant and onerous.

The traditional authoritarian approach which provided im-
mutable 'facts' served industrial society well. It provided not
only the 'facts' necessary for operating in a simpler society; it
also provided the socialisation for national, industrial conform-
ity. In the post-industrial education system, the authoritarian
approach will be negated by the need for a more versatile, self-
reliant population. Another reason for shifting from a central
authoritarian to an exploratory mode is to exploit the student's
own interests. Interest is probably the most important single
factor favouring learning.

The expansion of information will make it increasingly difficult for teachers to keep up with new developments. At the same
time it will allow students to become 'experts' at a much earlier
age. As a result of the decentralisation and democratisation of
education, there will be increasing reliance on students teaching
students, and students teaching teachers. The common effort of
exploring new knowledge can be extremely rewarding. It is
probably very much more efficient as a method of effective
learning than the traditional hierarchical one-way approach
which is the basis of contemporary education.

Knowledge may be defined as organised information. In the
past two centuries a whole host of new disciplines have prolifer-
ated. These tend to organise knowledge in what might be called
a vertical fashion. What is desperately needed now is the emergence of professional generalists (in contrast to professional
specialists) capable of organising knowledge along horizontal

lines. Such integrators of knowledge are still rare in education circles. Professionalism is associated with specialisation, which attracts a degree of snobbish appeal (bred by ignorance about the nature of knowledge). The difference between a professional and a lay person is that the professional is able to understand relationships which escape the lay person. It is as professionally challenging and difficult to establish relationships across disciplines as it is to establish them within specialisations. In fact, the case could be made that it is more difficult and therefore requires a higher degree of professionalism to be a generalist.

How will all this be paid for? At this point the reader may begin to worry about the financial resources required to achieve the transition. The UK's education budget towards the end of the 1970s was about £8.5 billion. North Sea oil revenues are expected to reach, then shortly exceed, that level in the mid-1980s. Assume that we spend most of this oil revenue on education. Also assume that the increase in the education budget is aimed particularly at the 16 to 22 age group to assure them an advanced education. Less than a quarter of this age group is in full-time higher education now. Assuming that this figure is doubled, it would mean that of the order of 500,000 additional youngsters would be placed in the education system. In 1977–8 over 700,000 teachers and lecturers were employed in the UK with another 500,000 employed as supporting staff (*CSO Social Trends*, 1980). It is not unreasonable to state that a doubled education budget would provide employment for at least a million people, especially since large numbers of people employed in education work part-time. Add to this number the 500,000 additional students in higher education kept out of the job market, and it is not unreasonable to assume that the number of registered unemployed would fall by about 1.5 million. At £5,000 per person unemployed, this would represent a saving to the government of £7.5 billion, almost as much as was spent in the first place. These savings should be ploughed into R & D to generate the wave-power electricity, the Severn barrage and other revenue-producing schemes which would also employ hundreds of thousands of workers, reducing unemployment costs still further. Thus there is created a productive, revenue-creating economy which allows further productive expansion along the lines indicated in previous sections.

Ah, but what happens when the oil runs out in the early 1990s? It is not at all probable that it will have run out by then. However, let us assume that it has. The answer lies in the reasonable expectation that by then the government should be collecting revenue from electricity generated by the new wave-power devices, and the entire level of economic activity should have returned to a level of buoyancy which makes the 1950s and 1960s look like small potatoes. Such an economy should provide close to 100 per cent employment and ample revenue for the government. Britain, because of the North Sea oil, is incredibly lucky. The international financial community understands this. Most Britons still do not understand. They are incredulous when the rest of Europe seems a bit resentful. Most Britons also do not understand that, were it not for North Sea oil, all that talk of leaving the EEC would be muted to a small lunatic fringe.

12　Recommendations: III Research

'... the invention of all those machines by which labour is so
much facilitated and abridged, seems to have been originally
owing to the division of labour. Men are much more likely to
discover easier and readier methods of attaining any object,
when the whole attention of their minds is directed towards
that single object, than when it is dissipated among a great
variety of things.'

Adam Smith, Book One, Chapter I.

In Adam Smith's day there was very little formal research and
development activity in the sense of having individuals or whole
teams of people employed full-time. It is not surprising, therefore, that the closest Adam Smith comes to discussing research
and development is in passages like the above. The innovations
of his time were made by a host of individual inventors who
pottered and tinkered away trying out this, then that, until they
perfected some invention. Organised industrial research, or for
that matter academic research, was in its infancy. No wonder
Smith attributed the technological advances of his day simply
to the fact that the division of labour focussed men's minds on
their speciality, and failed to see its importance in creating
wealth.

We have come a long way from Smith's world. Basic research,
applied research and development, leading to discovery, invention, innovation, and marketable product – these are all highly
institutionalised activities relying on high-salaried professionals
(high-level information operatives) for their success. In general,
the government must finance directly most of the research,
particularly basic research, while the commercial development
will be carried out by the private sector or by nationalised
industries. As Professor Ernest Braun, head of the University of
Aston's Technology Policy Unit, has pointed out, government

can stimulate the pace of innovation in at least four ways: by influencing the general environment where the innovators operate; by influencing industrial performance; by stimulating innovation in general; and by stimulating a specific innovation.

It is a sad fact of life that one of the first budgets slashed in any company which feels imperilled by a recession or other economic adversity is its R & D budget. Yet no company can remain viable for long in a high-technology information economy, if it does not continue to advance either in its product, or in the technology of creating that product. To cut R & D may, therefore, stabilise its finances today only to put it out of business tomorrow. Furthermore, unlike many other types of operations, it can take years before an effective research team develops. If there exists an effective team of scientists and engineers, start-up time on a new project may take only days to weeks, but to build up such a team, in the first place, may take years.

The government can help to ensure that private (and, for that matter, public) firms maintain a strong R & D effort, by such means as tax incentives, contracts and direct grants. To provide a specific example: a shipbuilding firm can lay off its yard workforce for a time, then pick up again as orders pick up. The same cannot be said for its engineering team. What a boon it might have been for Harland and Wolffe in Belfast, for example, to have a large government engineering contract in the late 1970s, to design and develop certain categories of electricity-generating wave-power devices. Every one of the wealth-generating private sector industries mentioned in chapter 10 needs government aid to achieve its full potential.

The last thing the government should be doing is inhibiting the development process, as for example, it was doing for a while in preventing British Telecom from borrowing money to develop its various advanced products.

In addition the public must be clear why the government is *the* institution to support basic research. Good research cannot be turned on and off like a water tap. The payback on basic research varies from years to generations. The same may be said for the training of scientists and research engineers. Only the very largest of companies can afford to invest over so long a period.

Why bother with research as basic as all that? Because without it one creates a shallow intellectual infrastructure, too shallow to ensure the technological leadership and problem-solving capability required for sustaining a post-industrial economy. As pointed out in the first chapter, the shift from an industrial to a post-industrial economy involves shifting from labour-intensive to knowledge-intensive industries. The fountainhead of new knowledge is research. In general, the more radically new the knowledge is, the more basic has been the research on which that new knowledge is based.

Just as most firms cannot afford the capital outlay for engaging in basic research, so can national governments ill afford to maintain, on their own, certain expensive types of research projects. This is particularly true for areas such as sub-atomic physics, space exploration, or projects involving the Antarctic, the oceans, the geosphere, etc. These projects become much more cost-effective when organised on a multinational basis. The long-term benefits, in terms of new sources of energy, materials and foodstuffs, are incalculable – partly because the effects are often so indirect. What, for example, would be the benefit to the British economy if we could develop a system of accurate global long-term weather forecasting?

WAVE POWER

Generating electricity from waves is of particular importance to the UK. The government should provide expenditures equal to at least the cost of a single nuclear power plant. If the project were conducted jointly with the Irish Republic, EEC funds could be made available as well. Contracts should be funnelled to engineering groups associated with shipbuilding, with Northern Ireland, Scotland, Tyneside and Liverpool receiving the largest share. Any group, university, government or private person or company with a good idea should be funded, including, in particular, hiring young scientists and engineers to work out the problems. The government should sponsor national prize-winning competitions for sixth-formers, teachers, inventors and scientists with substantial rewards, not only to generate new ideas, but to create excitement and focus public thought on the matter. The government should also create studentships and post-doctorate research assistantships in institutions of higher learning, with a view to producing a whole new generation of wave-power engineers and scientists, who will design and service the UK systems, then find contract employment around the world.

CONVERTING COAL TO OIL AND OTHER CHEMICALS

Here the research is developing so rapidly in other parts of the world that the National Coal Board should make certain as to what is happening elsewhere and ascertain where there are holes in the relevant technology which need to be filled. Also it needs to adapt foreign technology to British standards and requirements. The government must help formulate a timetable so that as North Sea oil and gas runs out there is ample time to switch to coal and other energy sources. This involves setting up pilot plants to obtain practical experience. Crucial in this process is the development of a trained cadre of scientists, engineers and managers who would have no difficulty in establishing and running new systems. Actually, government policy in this area appears to be adequate for the early 1980s.

RESEARCH AND DEVELOPMENT IN OTHER AREAS

Single-cell protein is moving, albeit slowly, of its own accord. The government should help by means of field testing, trying alternative production methods, grants and incentives and facilitating a healthy market for the product. The government should engage in a policy of increasing cheese (and biscuit) manufacture with a particular emphasis on overseas advertising and marketing. The government must also establish monitoring units to ascertain the environmental impact including any possible negative consequences upon the human or animal physiology.

Coastal fish-farming requires a lot of government support to

universities, polytechnics and research institutions to develop
the ecological understanding required for commercial coastal
fish-farming in cold water. In certain instances it becomes practical to heat the water, for example, by means of waste heat
from power plants. In other instances it may be necessary to
heat the water only during certain times of the year and this
may be achieved by trapping sunshine or utilising heat-gener-
ating wave-power devices. In general, however, it is by judi-
ciously creating productive marine ecosystems using perhaps
fish, algae and shellfish bred specifically to produce high yields
in a manner analogous to our terrestrial farming practices.
Again, it is no use producing a lot of whitefish, kelp, mussels or
whatever if there is no market. Improved canning and refrigeration techniques, as well as coupling the seafood to other products (such as fish and chips or deep-fried prawn and coleslaw)
will require further research. All will require help with overseas
marketing.

Freshwater fish-farming also needs help. Apart from substantially increasing its financial aid, one of the most useful things
the government can do is to remove the numerous legal and
administrative blocks presently encountered by fish-farmers.
Fish-farming is neither farming nor fishing and is always falling
between two stools. Liabilities for rates and water charges,
VAT, property rights, planning consent, environmental impact, grant aid, etc., all confuse and confound the entrepreneur
and add to cost. We need a national fish-farming policy. The
food production techniques should be extended deep into the
oceans. The development of kelp/fish-farms deserves further
support. Here it becomes important to settle 'law of the sea'
problems. The world's oceans should be developed with some
benefit to the whole of humanity by ceding 'high-seas property'
rights to the United Nations and leasing from them pieces of
territory.

Energy extraction and deep-ocean mining need to be supported as well. Production costs drop as more and more equipment is located on the sea bed. The trouble with manganese
nodule mining is that the leading companies around the world,

as with most new technologies, have no strong tradition of research and development work in this area. It is too long a shot – too much of a gamble. This is where government backing becomes crucial. The UK is not doing very much. In contrast, German companies have had up to 60 per cent of their costs paid by the government, while French companies have been receiving a 50 per cent subsidy.

Other service sector technologies include the whole area of telecommunications, computerisation and office development discussed previously. Britain could also make a substantial contribution in the field of bio-medicine. From new techniques for patching up the maimed victims of violence in Belfast, to experiments in genetic engineering, the UK has substantial expertise. Health care is one of the major economic growth areas, particularly in the post-industrial sector of the globe. Clearly there is a substantial economic opportunity here. The government should not only expand basic research in this area but also help entrepreneurs who wish to apply this theoretical base to specific products and services designed to alleviate sickness and suffering.

Without going into further detail, it must become clear that the British government needs a Ministry of Science and Development whose main function is to solve the problem of how best to convert economic non-resources into wealth-generating resources. One of its first jobs would be to make an accurate assessment of the nature and amount of R & D carried out by both the public and the private sectors. This survey needs to be done in any case in order to focus government and public attention on the whole question of how much money should be spent on R & D and in which areas.

Such a new ministry should move very cautiously about transferring R & D out of existing departments. Many forms of research are carried out better within the departments which use them, e.g. Agriculture or Health. However, the new Ministry of Science should provide a critical assessment and monitor both the quality of the work and the objectives of the project, as well as provide significant support. Such support should include

THE WEALTH OF INFORMATION

outright financial grants and help in making available expertise and specialised equipment or facilities. It should also aid information flows to and from the project. The main function of this ministry, however, would be to develop new food, energy and materials resources which could be harnessed for human welfare and to support research at all levels.

Britain is no longer the industrial workshop of the world. It does not matter if it stops making a lot of steel, cars or ships. It does not matter, economically speaking, if it makes none of these and imports them all. It matters no more than the fact that Britain imports all its tea and coffee. It could even afford to import all its computers if it is possible to train the appropriate technologists and experts. There are only two major problems if Britain de-industrialises: the loss of jobs and the loss of foreign exchange earnings. Both of these problems will evaporate once a strong post-industrial, information-based economy has developed. The function of government is to accelerate this process.

13 Towards the future

'The annual produce of the land and labour of England ...
is certainly much greater than it was, a little more than a
century ago, at the restoration of Charles II ... The annual
produce of the land and labour of England, again, was certainly much greater at the restoration, than we can suppose
it to have been about a hundred years before, at the accession
of Elizabeth. At this period, too, we have all reason to believe,
the country was much more advanced in improvement than
it had been about a century before, towards the close of the
dissensions between the houses of York and Lancaster. Even
then it was, probably, in a better condition than it had been
at the Norman Conquest, and at the Norman Conquest than
during the confusion of the Saxon Heptarchy. Even at this
early period, it was certainly a more improved country than
at the invasion of Julius Caesar, when its inhabitants were
nearly in the same state with the savages in North America.'
Adam Smith, Book Two, Chapter III.

This is how Adam Smith saw the progression of history – the
bettering of the human condition. It takes no great scholarship
to ascertain that the progress in the material condition of
humanity has continued to improve since Smith's time, and
that it has done so by leaps and bounds. Nor, barring a nuclear
disaster or some comparable catastrophe, does it take much
imagination to expect this process to continue, and to do so at
an accelerating pace. It is the pace which is so incredible. Our
children will live in a world of peace and plenty unprecedented
in recorded human history.

FORECASTING
The critical test of whether one truly understands a system is
one's ability to predict its behaviour. For example, understand-

ing our solar system allows astronomers to predict not only events obvious to our experience, such as the daily rising of the sun or the variations in seasons, but also unusual events such as the appearance of eclipses and comets, and events outside the realm of ordinary sensory experience such as those leading to the discovery of the planet Pluto.

We are still a long way from completely understanding our social systems. Nevertheless, our analysis of human social systems does allow a significant degree of social forecasting. This analysis must consider variation and selection at various levels of organisation ranging from the individual to global society. Societies have changed, evolved, with time from the hunter-gatherers to our information-oriented, post-industrial society. The driving force causing evolution is the self-reinforcing process of learning. The more that is known and the more that has been invented, the greater the opportunities for knowing and inventing. As our understanding grows and as technology extends our capabilities, our forecasting will become more accurate, and the ability to shape our destiny more real.

Note the use of the term 'forecasting' at this point to distinguish it from the more rigid implications of the term 'prediction'. A prediction states, 'Thus and so will happen.' A forecast states, 'If such and such is true, then the following will happen.' Forecasts present options, but give a higher degree of probability to one (or more) sets of expected events. There are many techniques for anticipating the future, among them one may include the following.

Goal-oriented future planning
This involves processes engaged in by virtually everybody. However, long-term planning covering several decades is practised most extensively by ambitious youths of the middle class: 'If I get good marks in school, then I'll be able to go to such and such a university. If I get to that university and do well and get such and such a degree I will be able to go on to such and such profession. If I become such a professional, I will go to London to practise, or I will join this or that firm and become an officer

by the time I'm forty. . . .' And so on. It is individual planning, engaged in by individuals who live in a highly structured advanced society which provides a wide variety of options. If a society provides no options for an individual, then clearly such goal-oriented planning makes no sense. This type of goal-oriented planning has a large element of forecasting in it. 'If I achieve this … then thus and so will happen. . . .' This is in contrast to prediction, i.e. processes which say: 'This will happen.' Goal-oriented future planning may also be engaged in by a variety of groups such as city planners and economic advisers.

Alternative future scenarios

This has become increasingly used by strategic military planners, and more broadly and less grimly by others concerned with future options for society such as environmentalists and students of the future. A series of alternative futures is imagined and judged in terms of desirability and practicality. Goal-oriented planning then devises steps for achieving (or avoiding) specific scenarios.

Astrology and other forms of superstition

Goal-oriented future planning makes sense only in a stable society providing numerous options, and only when engaged in by stable individuals free of excessive stress. Under stress, we tend to regress into one of the most primitive forms of mental activities … simple associations which have been positively or negatively reinforced. We associate a fortunate event with a set of circumstances leading up to it. This includes relevant and irrelevant factors such as wearing a particular necktie, being careful not to walk on the cracks in the pavement, rubbing a lucky penny, carrying a charm in one's pocket. These associations are greatly strengthened by the authority of folklore: walking under ladders, the number 13 or crossing the paths of black cats are bad. Giving a penny to a cripple, the number 7 or owning a black cat is good. In our anxiety to avoid future catastrophes, we obey the rules of a game we do not understand … but then we do not understand the vagaries of Fate either.

It is a simple step, in our fearful ignorance, to consult the official practitioners of the art ... crystal ball gazers, soothsayers, tea-leaf readers, palmists, hexocologists. ... The most venerable of these being, of course, the astrologer.

Intuitive prophesy

We are the possessors of an extraordinary device – the human brain. This highly sophisticated thinking machine is able to achieve intuitions and insights by combining information inputs with its stored memory. Some of this stored information may involve years of experience. The thinking processes involve factors frequently below the level of consciousness. All of us have intuitive feelings about the future in general and about specific future events. These 'feelings' about the future may be classed as prophecy, and frequently generate emotional states fluctuating from anxiety and depression, to euphoria. The pessimist is associated with the former, the optimist with the latter. Most of us engage in a mix of these feelings.

Inspired prophecy

The accuracy of a prophecy is a function of the sophistication and talent of the prophet. Sometimes an intuitive prophecy is so inspired it appears to be a vision. Such an inspired perception of future developments frequently articulates a popular yearning. A prophecy such as 'They shall beat their swords into ploughshares ...' may become so compelling that people start to work for it. This is how it may become a self-fulfilling prophecy. We shall expand on this process later.

Consensus prophecy

Our own feelings about the future are a reflection of the general feelings about the future shared by the members of the group to which we belong. Certainly the general consensus reinforces our own views.

Delphi studies

This is a more sophisticated form of consensus prophecy relying on 'experts' which tries to avoid the influence upon each individual by the group's general feelings about the future. Each expert is queried about the future independently. This technique is being used increasingly by business and other organisations in order to achieve an informed consensus about the future.

Trend extrapolation

This is one of the most widely practised forms of both common and 'scientific' forecasting. For example, by plotting the increase in the numbers of cars on the roads over the past ten years, experts extrapolate to a situation ten years hence, then apply this projection to plan road construction. Although this method is slightly more sophisticated than a qualitative guess about the future, trend forecasting when applied to complex systems is fallacious and misleading. One cannot predict tomorrow's weather simply by saying it was sunny the day before yesterday, yesterday and today, therefore it will be sunny tomorrow. There are reasonably reliable ways of forecasting the weather, but simple trend extrapolation is not one of them.

Ironically, trend extrapolation tends to dominate our thinking about the future. It manifests itself in terms of mass euphoria or hysteria about economic conditions. When things are going well, everybody acts and looks to the future as though the boom will last indefinitely. Then, when there finally is a recession, there develops a pessimism and hopelessness that things will keep on sliding downhill, which is equally misleading. Given the history of western economies, one would predict a rising, though irregular curve. However, intuitive thought mechanisms have difficulty extrapolating anything other than straight lines. So we resort to the short-term trend: we are either going up or going down.

This inability to intuit anything other than linear extrapolations leads to another form of misperception of the future: we tend to overestimate the rate of progress in the short run and underestimate it in the long run. Growth and development, particularly of technology, involve an exponential progression. When projecting into the future, we understand in an abstract way that the rate of change will increase over what it is at present. However, our intuition works lineally. What happens is that we try to average the rate of change.

Thus, when we perceive new technological breakthroughs, we are inclined to overestimate the rate of development over the next decade, but tend to underestimate substantially the rate of development over several decades. These statements apply only to those situations where the system, in fact, follows such an exponential progression. Clearly any extrapolation is likely to be misleading when the root cause of the trend involved is not understood. Trend extrapolation is able to predict neither changes in the trend nor the appearance of discontinuities brought about by new inventions or other circumstances.

Dynamic modelling

This is a more sophisticated form of trend extrapolation which involves multi-dimensional extrapolations. For example, if one looks at the future of energy consumption one may project the future not only in terms of a single component such as oil consumption or coal consumption, but as a mix of these, plus all the others including those future forms of energy for which some sort of prediction may be made. Among the most elaborate and sophisticated projections of this type is the Limits to Growth study performed by the Massachusetts Institute of Technology group. This type of forecasting is more reliable than single trend extrapolations because the vagaries of individual components may cancel each other out within the many dimensions of the computer-aided projections. However, if the model is merely based on past experience rather than on a true understanding of the systems involved, it is still likely to be fallacious and may lead to serious misperceptions of the future.

Input–output theory

This method predicts the impact on one part of an economic system as a result of making changes in another part of the system. It begins to achieve a much higher degree of reliability because it is based on a description of the system as a whole in

which an effort has been made to define precisely the inter-
actions of its components. The method has been applied to
studying ecosystems as well. Even though this technique does
not allow much leeway in terms of forecasting the development
of the system as a whole, at least it begins to allow reasonably
accurate predictions about the behaviour of parts of the system
in response to altering other parts of it. This type of methodology
is obviously a significant step forward in the science of forecasting. It reflects the beginning of a series of techniques which
ultimately should allow us to engage in scientific forecasting
within complex systems, including human social systems.

Monitoring 'indicators' of trends of change

The use of indicators for making predictions is still in its infancy.
One of its most successful applications has been in predicting
elections before and after the voting has taken place, with the
latter being, needless to say, more accurate. In the US, with
only a very small percentage of the final vote in, it is now
possible to predict, within very close limits, the outcome of an
election. It is by accurately assessing the significance of samples
(based on past experience) in reflecting the overall voting patterns which, coupled with computers, makes it possible to engage in a sophisticated trend extrapolation. As long as historical
experience continues to reflect voting patterns, such predictions
will continue to be reliable. The predictions do tend to be more
reliable by being multi-dimensional: even if, for example, the
Italian vote sample shifts in its attitude in one direction, the
farm block sample may shift in the opposite. Thus there may be
enough compensatory shifts among the various voting samples
for the overall outcome to remain the same.

Systems analysis and forecasting

This is best illustrated by weather forecasting. Tomorrow's
weather is not predicted by extrapolating from yesterday's.
Rather, the weather is forecast on the basis of looking at an
atmospheric system. This requires understanding a whole series
of phenomena. Under what circumstances is precipitation

likely, and in what form? At what rate are clouds likely to be moved by the upper layers of the atmosphere? By monitoring barometric pressures, by using satellite photographs of cloud formations, by determining wind velocities at various altitudes and by monitoring other indicators of weather, it becomes possible to make reasonably reliable forecasts of what will happen tomorrow in a complex system. We are still not able to extend weather forecasting for more than a few days except in those parts of the world where weather patterns are extremely stable and repetitious. However, as the science of meteorology progresses, as new techniques and new understanding of the systems becomes available, we can look forward to improvements in this field.

It is absurd to say we are not able to predict or forecast future events. We can predict eclipses with accuracy, we can predict with reasonable accuracy the outcome of an election once a few per cent of the election results are in, we can forecast tomorrow's weather reasonably well.

The more complex the system, the more difficult it is to understand it, the more difficult the forecaster's job. But it is not impossible. One of the best examples of an accurate forecast involving a complex situation is the one made by J. De Bloch at the turn of the century about World War I. His six-volume analysis of the industrial-military might of various European powers in the 1890s, coupled with his profound understanding of the technological developments of the time, provided a sound understanding of the war system as it had developed by then. At the turn of the century, generals and military experts viewed war on the basis of Germany's quick wars with Denmark, Austria and France in the 1860s and 1870s. This was a typical case of trend projection. In contrast De Bloch, whose forecasts were based on his exhaustive studies of the state of military affairs, predicted a long, protracted struggle with the outcome determined by which side's industrial capacity would collapse first. De Bloch also predicted trench warfare, stating that the shovel would become as important as the gun.

Normative planning

What will happen in the future is to some extent determined by what we would like to happen. Contrast the prediction of an eclipse with planning out a garden. An eclipse may be predicted with great accuracy, but we cannot do anything about it. In contrast, the fate of a garden is nowhere near as certain, but we can do a lot about it.

The great advances in science and technology allow us to produce exotic tropical gardens in arctic climates (or tundra ecosystems in the tropics). Adversities of climate can be countered with artificial heating or cooling. Similarly, lighting regimes can be altered, humidity controlled, fertilisers and in-secticides applied, while we can create whole new races of plants by means of artificial pollination and hybridisation. All these and other techniques give us the tools to make a garden grow the way we want it to. It has become possible to forecast the future of a garden in terms of what we would like to happen.

Our vision of a beautiful garden is determined by our sense of aesthetics – our sense of what is right and wrong, desirable and undesirable – our 'norms'. Hence the importance of taking into consideration our sense of values in forecasting the future. The shape of the future is determined, at least in part, by normative considerations: by the standards of what we would like to happen. The trouble is that improving social systems is much more difficult than growing a garden. In our ignorance we are like early Paleolithic hunters let loose on a garden: pulling up the crops and nursing the weeds, trampling the roses and protecting the brambles, killing the ladybirds and leaving the aphids. No one planned the Industrial Revolution. No one predicted micro-processors. In the name of making it a better world, children were brutalised in the early stages of the former, and young unemployed shut out from society during the advent of the latter. Our understanding of social and economic forces making up human societies is as primitive as was our under-standing of infectious diseases in the middle of the eighteenth century. It is the height of folly to believe that we understand society as we do our garden, and therefore that we can will the future – that relatively simple measures will yield us peace and justice and food for all.

In this book, the assessment of the future comprises a mix of several of the methods described above. The basic theory involves the concept that human social systems are derived from the primate social systems which preceded them. These systems, in turn, were determined by the interaction between society and the environment. This interplay became, and continues to become, altered by technology. Thus the hominid societies, through the use of weapons, expanded their activities to include hunting. The domestication of plants and animals, in turn, totally altered the relationship to the environment, with corresponding changes in social organisation and life-styles. The main driving force in human social evolution always was, and continues to be, advances in technology. However, technology itself comprises an evolving system. Thus, the emphasis on physical technology has been displaced by an emphasis on information technology. No longer does technology develop on an empirical basis – on mere trial and error – rather, it depends on the application of theory. To understand the future of society, we must look to the emergence of powerful new technologies, in particular meta-technologies. And to understand the future of technology, we must look to its fountainhead – developments in basic science.

These insights must ultimately be processed in a dynamic model. Unfortunately, for the time being, they can only rely on intuitive prophecy. Yet we learn. Each year we know more. And the powerful new information technology will help solve problems at an unprecedented rate. To be able to simulate the economy on a computer, and judge the impact of various policy options, is but one example. No problem remains insoluble once one knows enough, and the areas under our control are extending all the time. This is why it is so important that we take into account the normative aspects of social forecasts: the yearning for peace and stability, justice and independence, a decent living standard for all.

PROBLEMS OLD AND NEW

The decade which spanned the mid-1960s to the mid-1970s saw the emergence of a public concern over a constellation of problems, which were perceived to threaten human survival. These problems included pollution, impending shortages of critical resources, overpopulation, nuclear annihilation and repression of personal liberties by increasingly centralised governments. Although these problems deserve continuing concern, their threat is declining under the impact of advances in science and technology and the emergence of new institutions and cultural patterns.

At the same time, a new set of problems has emerged. First and foremost are the economic problems which have brought about inflation and unemployment simultaneously. Left unchecked, these problems could destroy western democratic society. The second, not unrelated to western economic problems, are the economic problems of the Third World. Our approach to a post-industrial economy must be global. The third problem is psychological – how to adapt to the rapidly changing information environment.

ENVIRONMENTAL ACCOUNTING

By the late 1960s there had emerged in most of the western (OECD) countries an environment movement effectively articulating its concerns in three basic areas: pollution, potential resource shortages and overpopulation. Pollution was affecting the air, water and land with a variety of man-made, or 'man-caused, products such as industrial wastes, chemicals or sewage, by excessive fertilisation and DDT, or just plain litter. On a global scale, DDT, nuclear proliferation or atmospheric catastrophes threatened the world. Included among these were the destruction of the ozone layer, the possibility of an ice age from too much fine dust in the stratosphere, or conversely, too much carbon dioxide, creating a 'greenhouse effect' which would melt the polar ice caps, and a similar polar melt-out which could result if sufficient spills from oil tankers reached the polar caps. These concerns, representing a broader, global ecosystems approach, received much impetus by the publication of Rachel Carson's book *Silent Spring* in 1964. The second area of concern, shortages of critical resources, included minerals and fuel as well as clean air, water and good farmland. These concerns became systematised by the publication of *Limits of Growth* (Meadows *et al.*) while their potential reality was driven home dramatically by the Arab-imposed oil sanctions in late 1973. Finally, over-population as a threat was backed by statistics from the UN and other sources, and brought forcefully to the public attention by Paul Erlich.

Unlike the more traditional 'conservation movements', which date back to early in the Industrial Revolution and which involved mainly the rich, the environment movement became broadly based, though still primarily middle class. Its response to the combination of environmental threats can be summed up by E. F. Schumacher's phrase 'Small is beautiful', which served as a paradigm for a whole generation of students.

The environment movement was vital in bringing awareness and public pressure to bear on these three basic concerns. As a result, increasingly stringent legislation reduced air and water pollution and severely restricted the use of DDT. Nuclear energy developments slowed and increasing sums of money became available for developing alternative energy sources. At the same time, industry, government and individuals were mo-tivated to begin serious energy conservation schemes. In addi-tion to these victories, the environment movement could not have foreseen the further technological developments such as computer-based control systems which reduced the re-quirements for energy and materials. Nor were they able to predict the technologically feasible exploitation of undersea oil reserves and deep-ocean minerals. Under the impact of science and technology, the problems have receded in importance and the forecasted critical time-span has been pushed back. The breathing space has been enhanced by the fact that a number of western countries have achieved zero population growth.

This does not imply, by any means, that the problems are solved. Much work remains to be done. Along with the new knowledge of population dynamics and existing resources, technology must continue to explore alternative energy sources – solar, wave, coal, etc. Technology now involves substituting information for energy and materials; we have already discussed numerous examples, including the use of the telephone instead of the mail, or making visits, or reducing fuel consumption by micro-processor-controlled fuel injection systems in motor cars. Creating substitutes, such as coal processed into oil, or replacing copper cables with optical glass fibres, should be considered as prototypes for solving the problems of shrinking material resources. Similarly, we have discussed how technology can develop other new resources, including a vast expansion of food production in the form of fish-farming and desert greenhouses.

As a result of a massive expansion of productivity, sufficient wealth can be produced around the world to effect a demographic shift which would permit us to attain a stable population. That is, once a society becomes sufficiently affluent to afford a pension system so that old people no longer need depend on their children for financial support, improves agricultural productivity so that family child labour becomes irrelevant, and improves public health so that infant mortality becomes negligible, then, and only then, does family planning become practical. It is at this point that contraception, abortion on demand and economic incentives begin to make a real impact on population growth. A survey conducted in Japan in the 1950s reported that many families, when confronted with the choice of a third child or being able to afford a refrigerator chose the refrigerator. (This apparently was not true for a first child.) It is probably true to say that in the United States today the average family, given a choice between two children whom they can afford to send to university, and four children whom they can't, would choose the former. That is the mechanism of the demographic shift – to develop an economic base in which there is not only no need to have many children, but where it becomes a positive disadvantage. Once this happens, it takes less than a generation for customs and belief systems to change.

THE FUTURE OF WAR

The history of the world is punctuated with outbreaks of violence, at times terrible to behold. It seems that there is no limit to the ingenuity human beings are able to apply in doing each other in. Yet war is an institution on the demise. That ancient institution, first appearing in force with the rise of the ancient civilisations, no longer fulfils social needs and is disappearing in the post-industrial era, as slavery disappeared in the industrial era. The primary social need for war, the need to expand resources to match growing populations, is being met more effectively through technological ingenuity and relative population stability.

COMMUNICATION AND DEMOCRACY

Living in a post-industrial world means not only that we are more affluent, more resourceful and less likely to go to war, but also more likely to democratise. One reason for this tendency is the expansion of the physical communications system (more and more telephones, television stations, radio stations and publishers, etc.). The information system becomes even more leaky as a result of the incessant stream of foreign visitors flying in and out of a modern country. Second, and more important, there are the rising education levels and the increasing proportion of the labour force which can be classed as information operatives. During the normal course of their work peasants need not communicate with other peasants, although they may do so socially in the evening. Factory workers generally need not communicate with workers in other factories, except socially or to organise themselves for trade union purposes. However, in that latter capacity they are readily subject to surveillance. In fact one reason why it was so difficult early in the Industrial Revolution to organise workers was that the individuals engaged in such activities were almost immediately known to the employers and therefore could be punished or sacked.

In contrast, information operatives have to communicate with each other all the time in order to carry out their jobs. Information operatives are always calling each other on the telephone, writing each other memoranda, attending interminable conferences. That is the nature of the job. It becomes very difficult to monitor these activities. In fact in order to do so you need a police greater than the entire working population; obviously this is not economically possible. Therefore no dictator can survive for any length of time in communicative society as the flows of information can no longer be controlled from the centre. Too many people contribute significantly to the running of the highly integrated web of post-industrial economies – decision-making power has diffused out. Information is the new coin of power, just as money or ownership of land used to be. Widespread and advanced public education, plus massive communication networks (particularly television), which will shortly be coupled to new home-based electronic data systems, assure a further diffusion of information over the entire society. As more and more people go on to higher education, as the communications/information networks expand (including electronic polling techniques), as an increasingly complex economy requires more and more significant specialists' inputs, the society will continue to move towards consensus democracy. Orwell's *1984* paradigm does not portray what is happening. Television did not become a device whereby Big Brother spies on the people. Rather, television became a device whereby the people spied on their political leaders.

The countries to enter communicative society in the 1970s included the southern tier European countries: Greece, Portugal and Spain. The process will overtake most of the socialist bloc European countries, including the Soviet Union, during the 1980s.

TOWARDS A GLOBAL ECONOMIC ETHOS

The approach to a post-industrial economy must be global. Instead of the parochial and often fruitless attitude, 'We must be competitive in the world', often at the price of someone else's welfare, we need to develop an economic ethos centred on increasing global productivity as a whole – to everyone's benefit, including one's own country. The 'starving millions' must be made healthy and prosperous. When they are they also become good customers. A global economic ethos allows a country to consider its best contribution to the global economy based on its own resources, traditions and skills – its 'comparative advantage'. Such considerations tend to make it 'competitive' in a positive sense, for it is providing those goods and services most needed and therefore most likely to find world markets.

The reduction of the threat of war in the post-industrial society, coupled with the increasing tendency towards consensus democracy, is a result of our extending communication networks. Right now, however, such an optimistic picture is in direct contrast to what is happening in the Third World, which is presently moving from an agrarian base into an industrial phase. In the process, Third World societies will continue to show an increase in authoritarianism, nationalism, militarism, internal strife and international war. To compound the problem, the introduction of modern medicine has depressed death rates sufficiently to cause the population 'explosion' which, until it is countered by a marked rise in productivity, can only lead to further economic and political instabilities.

We, in the post-industrial society, must bring about a massive increase in productivity to provide economic stability to pull the rest of the world into the next phase of social evolution. There are powerful moral, economic and imperative reasons for this.

The moral reason stated simply is that it is wrong to allow people to starve when there is enough to go around. The economic reason is that there are about three billion poor people who are not participating properly in the global economy, who could be both good customers and producers of goods and services which would enhance the quality of life for everybody. The imperative reason is that until all nations have moved into post-industrial society the threat of a nuclear disaster hangs over all our heads. The rate at which the 'civilian' nuclear technology is spreading in the late 1970s and early 1980s makes it only a question of time before there will be a nuclear detonation. Most likely it will involve a conflict during the 1990s between two Third World countries, but there could also be a north/south confrontation arising out of Moslem nationalism, the conflict involving either the Soviet Union or the West or both allied against the Moslem states. In any case, poverty breeds both dictatorships and wars, and it behoves the 'haves' to help the 'have nots'.

But how?

We have already pointed to the adroit use of technology to develop coastal fish-farming, making the deserts bloom, solar photovoltaic cells, etc., to upgrade the Third World's resource base. There can be no question that the answer must rely largely on such developments. What is critical, however, is the speed at which new technology can be developed, introduced and assimilated. Here the limiting factor is not so much capital as know-how. Third World countries are often desperately short of personnel who possess the necessary technological and managerial skills. It is this information gap which needs to be closed. It is simply not true to say that the materials gap between the rich and the poor countries is widening. During the 1970s, while growth of the developed countries was decelerating, Third World growth remained stable and, more importantly, the Third World share of both world trade and output in manufacturing rose. The Third World countries with the greatest success were countries like Korea, Taiwan, Singapore and Hong Kong which either left, or will soon leave, their LDC status behind. These countries are noted for their highly skilled managerial and labour force. They managed to close the information gap.

A second group of Third World countries, belonging to OPEC, are resource-rich and have become capital-rich, but until they close the information gap, will continue to be classed as LDCs, highly dependent on oil for their continuing prosperity. However, most of these countries are busy importing technology and expanding their education systems so that by the 1990s they are likely to become developed countries themselves. The real long-term problem lies with countries which are trapped either by their scant physical resource base, or by their culture, into poverty and ignorance.

The limiting factor for global development lies in the rate at which new scientific and technological developments can come to the aid of the poorer countries. These developments must be viewed in terms of 'appropriate technology', that is, technology which fits into the local ecology, economy and culture. Paradoxically, the most advanced technology, micro-processors and photovoltaics, may turn out to be the most appropriate. These are decentralised, potentially low-cost technologies which could bring into every dwelling a source of energy and a source of information. However, the rate at which new technology is assimilated may well be determined by the level of education of a country's population. An ignorant population fails to appreciate the opportunities provided by new technology and therefore leaves the matter to others, often at its own expense. The limiting factor in global economic development will probably relate to the rate of global educational development. The use of micro-processors in education is just beginning, but by the 1990s will have become a potent force in educational technology. The information gap could be closed by bringing into every Third World home electronic education devices designed to provide relevant information on a wide range of subjects.

FUTURE SHOCK

Advancing science and technology change society. They change not only the physical basis of a society and its economy, but as a result (and sometimes directly) its mores, values and belief systems. To take one example, members of the 'old' school were appalled at the apparent lack of social responsibility manifested by the younger generation – a generation which rejected both the Protestant work ethic and pride in one's country.

The Protestant work ethic dates back to the early seventeenth century, a time when feudal power was being displaced by national power; and hereditary aristocratic power, in turn, was giving way to financial power. It had become posssible for a significant number of people actually to change their station in life by hard work. The promised land could be attained in this world if one were willing to give long-term rewards precedence over immediate gratification.

'Hard work' and 'planning for the future' and 'a penny saved is a penny earned' were rational strategies to guard against the 'rainy day'. Such values, which once served the middle classes of the industrial era, make little sense in the welfare state of the post-industrial era. The three main reasons for saving to prevent personal financial disaster – loss of employment, illness and retirement in old age – were problems mitigated by unemployment compensation, mortgage relief, hospitalisation insurance and pension plans. Only the spectre of the Great Depression of the 1930s still haunted some in the late 1970s. By the early 1980s the rapid rise in unemployment, coupled with other economic uncertainties, changed perceptions and attitudes, although this will be only temporary. New generation gaps will appear, and widen, as society moves further into the post-industrial economy.

It is highly probable that in hominid societies, the practice of food-sharing developed extensively. If this is true, then the human psyche would find it logical that a people should share what they have and, conversely, that an affluent society should automatically take care of all its needy members. The equitable distribution of wealth became a matter of increasing concern as society moved deeper into the communicative society. The re-examination of Marxist and neo-Marxist doctrines by students and others entering the post-industrial era, as well as the extension of the welfare state, raised great anxieties among those steeped in the work ethic.

The changes in social norms are now so rapid – the decline of old institutions, the emergence of new ones – that an entire generation is becoming culturally disoriented. This phenomenon has been termed 'future shock' by Alvin Toffler. In a more recent work, *Learning for Tomorrow*, Toffler and his co-authors suggest the remedy: the need for educating the young not merely for the future but for the changing future.

To cope with rapid change, we need to expand the education system to give our young the skills to anticipate the future and to adapt easily to change. This means an expansion of three areas in particular, technology, history and anthropology.

Technology, because one cannot understand human cultural evolution without it, nor anticipate the future; history because this provides both a sense of roots and a sense of change; and anthropology, because it examines the broad range of cultural responses possible to meet environmental, psychological and other needs. It becomes easier to adapt one's belief systems after studying those held by others. These three fields do not exhaust the areas of human knowledge of relevance to understanding the shape of the future. Obviously biology, psychology, sociology, economics, literature, etc. all have further contributions to make. However, in all instances, two fundamental changes need to be made in teaching: the courses must become interdisciplinary and future-oriented. Only that way can we come to comprehend the nature of the evolving system of which we are a part.

NEEDED: A SHIFT IN GOVERNMENT POLICIES

We may not be able to escape the laws of economics but, with luck, we may escape the dogmas of economists. The physiocrats did not understand the Industrial Revolution. Their economic doctrines did not adapt to the shift from an agrarian to an industrial economy. We are in the same predicament today. With minor (albeit significant) exceptions, economists seem to have failed to understand the full implications of the electronic and information revolutions which have taken the economy beyond material goods production. Their neo-physiocratic economic doctrines have not adapted to the shift from an industrial to an information economy. Hopefully this book will aid in the escape from neo-physiocrats. In any case, the pressure of unemployment will tend to favour those political forces prepared to use the public sector for expanding employment. At least some of that employment will be productive. As the concepts of what constitutes a post-industrial economy become clearer, new government policies should emerge to create wealth from proper investment in public-sector employment.

Most public expenditures are crucial for providing the economic infrastructure without which modern productive systems could not operate. Other expenditures clearly constitute investment. A post-industrial country's most important resource is its human capital – the skills and education of its people. It is people who create wealth. Any economic analysis which ignores this basic fact can only provide misleading conclusions. On the other hand, once this concept is clearly understood it sets the stage for the next constructive step.

The next constructive step involves the massive expansion of the education system, a step likely to be taken by most governments in the 1980s and 1990s. The question will not be whether to expand, but how. How does one expand the system in a way to guarantee social and economic payback? What is the best way to add value to human capital? Should the expansion of education take the form of state schools and universities only? Does it make sense to support independent institutions with public funds? Should the expansion involve only schools, universities and other institutions (either state or private), or should one expand the use of mass media in education such as 'Sesame Street' in the US and the Open University in the UK? What would be the consequences of the state providing every child, in its own home, with a computer centre and a 'grandmother'? How can one ensure that the improved levels of education provide both the wealth necessary to pay for the system and, at the same time, an enlightened citizenry capable of responding constructively and humanely to the stresses of change?

Unfortunately we have been ambiguous in our demands of education. Do we mean education? Or do we mean training? And how effective has the education system been in the past? By what criteria? Falling industrial share of the world market? Not enough innovation? Here one can only argue that British expansion of education was simply not enough, at least when compared with Japan or the US. Technological illiteracy among British management in both the private and the public sectors is shameful. Whereas an engineering degree is a major avenue to top management posts in the US, it appears to be a handicap in the UK.

The percentage of UK school-leavers going on to higher education must be doubled. Then doubled again. By early in the next century managers must, on average, have been exposed to about twenty years of formal education by the time they are 35 years old. That is, the equivalent of a Ph.D. Without such a powerful theoretical knowledge base, managers will not be able to function effectively in an advanced information economy.

The difference between professional training and general education must also be understood. A complex society cannot be run by people who received only specialist training. All citizens must have been exposed to a good general education. Furthermore, the higher up on the decision-making hierarchy one is located, the broader must have been one's education. Increasingly we need people who have both a specialist training and a broad education. Higher education needs to be expanded enormously, as part of a cradle-to-grave system with individuals moving in and out of education throughout their lives. We need to enter into a great public discussion about what the new education system should look for and what it ought to accomplish. The shape of tomorrow's world is determined by today's education system.

BEYOND MATERIALISM

Economic history can be interpreted as an interplay between two major forces: the attempt to satisfy human needs and the ability to do so. Up to the early Paleolithic era the matter was no different from that which might be observed for other advanced mammals. Stable populations adapt to their environment, establishing an equilibrium with food resources, predators and disease. The late hominids were more successful than their primate cousins because their hunting technology provided them with a second major source of food, meat. As long as populations did not grow (or if populations did grow, there was sufficient new land to move to) resources were in line with needs. The hominid psyche had millions of years of evolution to adapt to the environment – and find joy in it.

Beginning with fire and language, right through to nuclear energy and computers, there appeared at various times during the natural history of humanity major new technologies which profoundly altered the equilibrium. Cultural evolution superceded biological evolution. Ten millenia after the Neolithic Revolution, the planet is overrun with humans. Virtually every kind of terrestrial habitat is occupied by them, while they crawl over the highest mountains, dive to the deepest oceans and now, beyond the earth, explore the moon and the planets. New technological developments have altered the existing equilibrium and provided new modes of production and new forms of social organisation. In addition, new technological developments alter human perceptions and expectations. We now live in a synthetic environment, both physically and socially. The psychological stresses are enormous. More than ever, the economies of the future will address themselves to the fulfilment of human psychological needs.

This fits in with a broad western historical trend. Over the past centuries there has been a shift in the main economic activities of society. Initially during the Agrarian era, the major preoccupation dealt with the production of food and other agricultural products. Judging from the frequency of famines sweeping western Europe, that problem was not solved until the technological advances of the mechanical era. European (and North American) societies assured of a bountiful food supply shifted their major economic activities to the production of a wide range of manufactured goods. The rise of the communicative era saw the shift to a service economy. The materials resource base of society had become reasonably secure – the main worry seemed to centre on excessive production capacity, rather than shortages of food, clothing, shelter or other goods. Thus, the major preoccupation of the post-industrial economy shifted to the production of information – information with which to solve production problems and extend society's resource base, as well as improve its organisation.

The shift to a service economy in the early communicative era included the rapid growth of education, social care and health care, both mental and physical. The expansion of these services took place in both the private and the public sector, indicating the growth of a new market. In a sense, there has appeared a new industry, the 'happiness industry', which includes most of those economic activities which do not provide materials or services related to materials production, i.e. to mere physical survival. Clearly the leisure industry belongs to the happiness industry, but so does a good part of education, health and social care. It is these areas which will become the most important areas of economic activity of the future as robotised systems secure materials production.

One can readily envision a negative income-tax system emerging, first in 1980 in the state of Alaska, then among OECD countries, finally on a global basis. As oil began to flow across Alaska so did the revenues from that oil. By 1980 that amounted to $3 billion. For the state government, that revenue was too large to absorb. Even after abolishing state income-tax and investing the surplus revenues in stocks and bonds and various enterprises, Alaska was left with an embarrrassing excess of funds. They voted, therefore, to award Alaskan residents $50 for each year lived and taxed in the state. As a result 270,000 Alaskans were awarded $1,000 each.

At the moment this Alaskan situation is regarded as a freak occurrence. It is not; it will happen more and more often as technology converts more and more non-resources into revenue-yielding resources. Sometime in the first quarter of the next century technological progress will have been enough to make worries about money less and less relevant. As more people come to perceive this altered state of affairs, they will generate political pressures to modify the current economic institutions.

History is filled with political conflict between people who wish to satisfy human needs, and people who do not believe that the existing resources can stand the strain of such programmes. Undoubtedly our Victorian forefathers would have been shocked at the idea of universal education until the age of 16. First they would have considered it immoral. Second they would have been convinced that it would bankrupt the country. They would have been right. It would have been immoral because it would have bankrupted the country. Early Victorian production capacity had not yet reached the level where it would have been practical to remove so large a percentage of the labour force from materials production. Similarly, the ideas of social security, unemployment compensation and nationalised health schemes all seemed radical when they were first proposed and fought for. People in favour of such wild ideas were branded as a threat to society and persecuted.

The idea that the government should disburse £250 per month to all adults, irrespective of their employment, would be considered immoral and impractical to most people today. They are right. With the exception of the state of Alaska and certain of the Arab oil-producing countries, it is impractical at this point in human history. And if it is impractical, if it bankrupts the country, it is immoral. But it is likely to become practical in the future. Early in the next century, as we gain the experience of successfully tapping new sources of energy, materials and food – as we discover how to automate virtually all materials-producing systems – we will learn to live off the backs of the robots as the ancient rulers lived off the backs of their slaves. Everyone an aristocrat. That is the shape of the future as far as materials satisfaction is concerned.

As our material resource base becomes sufficiently large to assure everyone a guaranteed annual income, our social and economic preoccupations will shift to fulfilling human psychological needs. What does it mean to be human? Assuming that we do not live by bread alone, just what does it take to make us happy?

The answers to these problems will come from many sources but surely two major scientific areas to shed light on this subject will be ethology and anthropology. The former, the biology of behaviour, when coupled with the more scientific aspects of psychology, will help unravel the biological programming of our psyche which began at least twenty million years ago – the reasons for the structure of our emotional makeup. Anthropology will provide insights about the enormous plasticity of human social organisation and the multiplicity of customs and institutions designed to solve psychological problems and fulfil human needs. It is here that the Third World societies will have much to contribute; for although they have much to learn from the West in respect to physical technology, the West has much to learn from them in terms of social technology.

To sum up, everyone an aristocrat, everyone a philosopher. A massively expanded education system to provide not only training and information on how to make a living, but also on how to live. In late industrial society we stopped worrying about food. In late communicative society we will stop worrying about all material resources. And just as the industrial economy eliminated slavery, famine and pestilence, so will the post-industrial economy eliminate authoritarianism, war and strife. For the first time in history, the rate at which we solve problems will exceed the rate at which they appear. This will leave us to get on with the real business of the next century. To take care of each other. To fathom what it means to be human. To explore intelligence. To move out into space ...

Bibliography

The information covered in this book comes from many sources. Most of the technical details come from academic and technical journals, reports and books, as well as the press, media, encyclopaedias, interviews and other sources.

The decision to make this a popular, rather than an academic, book meant that the information was digested in such a way as to preclude footnotes. Therefore the interested reader is referred to a limited number of books and sources which the author has found particularly helpful. This list is a very personal one and does not presume to cover the fields indicated – merely to provide the reader with a guide to further literature, a literature which influenced the author's own thinking.

Bell, Daniel, *The Coming of Post-Industrial Society*, Basic Books, New York, 1973.

Braun, Ernest and Stuart MacDonald, *Revolution in Miniature*, Cambridge University Press, 1978.

Evans, Christopher, *The Mighty Micro*, Victor Gollancz, London, 1979.

—— *The Making of the Micro*, Victor Gollancz, London, 1981.

Forester, Tom (ed.), *The Microelectronic Revolution*, Basil Blackwell, Oxford, 1981.

Friedrichs, Günter and Adam Schaff (eds.), *Microelectronics and Society*, Pergamon Press, Oxford, 1982.

Gosling, William, *The Kingdom of Sand*, Council for Educational Technology in the UK, 1981.

Jenkins, Clive and Barrie Sherman, *The Collapse of Work*, Eyre Methuen, London, 1979.

Keynes, John Marnard, *The General Theory of Employment, Interest and Money*, Harcourt, Brace, Jovanovich, New York, 1964.

Langrish, J. *et al.*, *Wealth from Knowledge*, Macmillan, London, 1972.

Large, Peter, *The Micro Revolution*, Fontana, 1980.

Machlup, Fritz, *The Production and Distribution of Knowledge in the United States*, Princeton University Press, New Jersey, 1962.

McHale, John, *The Changing Information Environment*, Westview Press, Colorado, 1976.

New Scientist magazine – provides frequent coverage of the development of microelectronics and computers, and many related issues.

Nora, Simon and Alain Minc, *The Computerization of Society*, MIT Press, Cambridge, Mass., 1981.

Pacey, Arnold, *The Maze of Ingenuity*, Holmes & Meier, New York, 1975.

Porat, Marc, *The Information Economy*, Centre for Interdisciplinary Research, Stanford University, 1976.

Scientific American magazine, which at least once a year features detailed, but well illustrated, articles on the development of microelectronics and computers; also covers many of the other technical topics discussed.

Smith, Adam, *The Wealth of Nations*, Edwin Cannan (ed.), University of Chicago Press, 1976; Books I–III, Andrew Skinner (ed.), Pelican Books, 1970.

Stonier, Tom, 'The Natural History of Humanity: Past, Present and Future' in *International Journal of Social Economics 7:* 3–11, 1980; also in *International Journal of Man-Machine Studies 14:* 91–122, 1981.

—— 'The third industrial revolution – microprocessors and robots' in *Microprocessors and Robots: Effects of Modern Technology on Workers*, International Metalworkers' Federation, Vienna, 1979.

—— 'Changes in western society: educational implications' in T. Schuller and J. Megarry (eds.), Kogan Page, London; also in Colin Richards (ed.), *New Directions in Primary Education*, Falmer Press, 1982.

—— 'The impact of microelectronics and related technology on the future' in J. R. Forrest (ed.), *Microelectronics – Advanced Technology for the Benefit of Mankind*, Proceedings, British Association for the Advancement of Science, London, 1979.

—— 'Technological change and the future' in Maxwell Gaskin (ed.), *The Political Economy of Tolerable Survival*, Croom-Helm, London, 1981.

—— (with P. Thornton), 'Forecasts of trends in the post-industrial society' in B. C. Twiss (ed.), *Social Forecasting for Company Planning*, Macmillan, London, 1982.

—— 'The emerging information society', Proceedings of the 9th Australian Computer Society Conference, 1982.

Toffler, Alvin, *Future Shock*, Bantam Books, New York, 1970.

Tourain, Alain, *The Post-Industrial Society*, Wildwood House, London, 1974.

US Department of Commerce/Office of Telecommunications, Special Publication 77-12, *The Information Economy: Definition and Measurement*, May 1977.

White, Lynn Jr, *Medieval Technology and Social Change*, Clarendon Press, Oxford, 1962.

STATISTICAL INFORMATION

Various sources, including:

Basic Statistics of the Community, 16th edition, Eurostat, 1978 (available from HMSO).

Facts in Focus, Penguin Books with HMSO.

Financial Times, which not only provides information, tables, graphs, etc. on a wide range of topics, but usually provides the source.

Statistical Abstract of the United States, US Department of Commerce, Bureau of the Census, Washington DC.

The United Kingdom Economy, Heinemann Educational, 1976.

United Kingdom in Figures (and other UK government statistics), HMSO.

Index